# PRACTICAL CHRISTIANITY

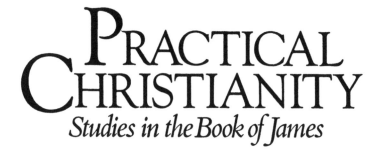

# PRACTICAL CHRISTIANITY
## Studies in the Book of James

# DAVID L. ROPER

Gospel Advocate Co.
P.O. Box 150
Nashville, TN 37202

Published by Gospel Advocate Co.
P.O. Box 150, Nashville, TN 37202

ISBN 0-89225-291-X

Dedicated to my father
DAVE H. ROPER
who loves the book of James
and who has taught me so much about the
PRACTICALITY of Christianity

# CONTENTS

Note:
Unless otherwise indicated, the King James Version (KJV) is used in these lessons. More common translations will be indicated by abbreviations: ASV (American Standard Version), NASB (New American Standard Bible), NKJV (New King James Version), NEB (New English Bible), NIV (New International Version), RSV (Revised Standard Version).

# "BE HAPPY!"

### James 1:1-4

Through the years there have been varied reactions to the book of James. Some have not cared for it. The book contradicted Luther's doctrine of "salvation by faith only," so he called it "a right strawy Epistle, for it has no true evangelical character." Some modern critics have dismissed it as a Jewish work, crudely altered by dishonest Christians in the 2nd or 3rd century.

But it is a marvelous book. Barclay says that when he started his commentary on James, he approached the book as a duty and found it a joy. J. W. Roberts called it "one of the finest and richest works of the New Testament." George Bailey notes that it can be read in a few minutes but thought of for a lifetime.

When you begin to study the book, you will find that there are many interesting things about it. For instance, there is its style. It has been called "the Christian book of Proverbs" as it moves quickly from one topic to another. Further, it achieves continuity by the use of an interesting literary device where a word at the end of one clause is repeated at the first of the next clause (see James 1:2-6). Then there is its distinctly Jewish flavor—as it refers to such things as the twelve tribes (James 1:1), the synagogue (James 2:2), the law (James 2:11), and Old Testament worthies (James 2:21, 25; 5:17) —while it remains Christian to the core. Of course the *most* interesting thing is that the book of James *is inspired of God* and given to help *us* (II Timothy 3:16, 17).

As an introduction to the book, in this lesson we will be studying the first four verses.

## I. JAMES WANTS US TO BE HAPPY.
## Verse 1.

The first verse is introductory: "James a servant of God and of the Lord Jesus Christ, to the twelve tribes which are scattered abroad, greeting." Let me summarize the verse by saying, *"James wants us to be happy."* The verse contains three parts:

### A. THE AUTHOR.

The author does not identify himself beyond calling himself "James." Apparently he was well-known and felt that this was sufficient for identification. We determine which James he was by the process of elimination.

There are only four Jameses mentioned in the New Testament. Two can be eliminated because they were *not* well-known (Luke 6:16; Mark 15:40). A third James, the apostle who was the son of Zebedee and brother of John, was well-known, but can be eliminated because he died a martyr's death under Herod Agrippa I very early—before the year A.D. 44 (Acts 12:2cf.). Who was left? James, the Lord's half-brother, who became a "pillar" of the church at Jerusalem. Identifying the exact James has nothing to do with the authenticity of the book, or the fact that it is from God, but it is a matter of some interest.

James, the Lord's half-brother, would have written from a unique vantage point. For a few minutes let us survey his life. It is a thrilling story as he moves from unbelief to faith.

The little home at Nazareth was well-filled. According to Matthew 13:55, 56 there were Joseph, Mary, Jesus, four brothers, and at least two sisters—at least *nine* people in that humble home. Of course, James and the other brothers and the sisters were only *half*-brothers and *half*-sisters of Jesus since they had the same mother (Mary), but not the same father (God was Jesus' father; Joseph was the father of the rest).

Since James is always listed first in the list of Jesus' half-brothers, he was probably the oldest, next to Jesus. Think of him as just a little younger than Jesus and growing up in the same environment. It also might not be out of the way to think of that touch of resentment that the second oldest often feels for the oldest.

Basically, however, there seems to be congeniality in the family circle, even when Jesus left home to start preaching (John 2:12). But then reports started filtering back that Jesus claimed to be the Son of God—and He claimed to perform miracles. "My big brother has gone crazy!" must have been the thought that entered James' mind and the minds of others of Jesus' family and friends (Mark 3:21, 31). The family traveled south to find Him and bring Him home (Mark 3:31-35). This is when Jesus said: "Who is my mother, or my brethren? . . . For whosoever shall do the will of God, the same is my brother, and my sister, and mother" (verses 33-35).

No doubt James felt this rebuff keenly. Then, following this, Jesus "had the nerve" to come to Nazareth (where James would have been still living) and claim to be the Messiah (Matthew 13:54-58)! When the people didn't believe Him, Jesus left, but James would have had to live day after day with the taunts about his "lunatic brother." Perhaps it is not surprising that the younger brothers (James as the oldest would probably have been the spokesman) taunted Jesus one day about showing off His "powers" in Judea (John 7:2-4). John 7:5 says plainly, "For neither did his brethren believe in him." Intimacy does not always breed understanding—and familiarity often does breed contempt.

What a sad scene it was when Jesus on the cross did not feel that He could commit the care of His mother to the next oldest, James (John 19:26cf.), probably because James was so totally out of sympathy with all for which Jesus stood.

*But then something happened!* We often speak of the dramatic conversion of Saul and the turnabout in his life, but the change in James is no less dramatic. What is the turning point? When Paul is listing the *resurrection* appearances of Jesus, he mentions the appearance to the five hundred, and then says, "After that he was seen of James" (I Corinthians 15:7a). James must have been very special to Jesus.

From that point on, James' progress in the faith is remarkable.

When the disciples were waiting in Jerusalem for the coming of the Holy Spirit, James and his brothers joined their number (Acts 1:13, 14). Don't you know they received the heartiest of welcomes?!

As time went by, James grew in the faith. Finally he emerged as a figure of prominence in the church at Jerusalem (Acts 12:17). Three years after Paul's conversion, Paul spoke of visiting with "James, the Lord's brother" (Galatians 1:19). Fourteen years later, James was referred to by Paul as one of the "pillars" in the church at Jerusalem (Galatians 2:9). At the so-called "Jerusalem conference," James was one of the principal spokesmen (Acts 15:13ff.). In the New Testament, James is *not* referred to as "the bishop of the church at Jerusalem," but he *did* become a very influential member (Acts 21:18).

Something of James' later years is given by various historians. James came to be known as a man of great piety, commanding the respect of Jews and Christians alike. He was called James "the Just" because of his sincerity and honesty. It is said that his knees became as calloused as those of a camel because of his constant kneeling in prayer.

Ultimately, however, he incurred the wrath of the rich and corrupt leaders of the Jews and they sought to discredit him. They called on him to deny that his half-brother was actually the Messiah, the Son of God, but instead he boldly and loudly confessed the faith that he once denied. This enraged his tormentors, and using the excuse that he was a breaker of the Law, they threw him down from the temple, stoned him, and then finished him off with a club. According to one writer, James died with a prayer on his lips for his murderers.

An exciting story!

But to return to more mundane things: If James, the half-brother of the Lord, is the author, this also tells us something of the *time, place,* and *situation* of the writing:

The place of the writing was probably Jerusalem.

The time of the writing would be between A.D. 44 when this James came to prominence (after the death of James, son of Zebedee) and A.D. 62, the approximate time this James died. *The book of James may be the first written of all the books in the New Testament.*

The situation is the oppressive period under the High Priest, Ananias, who had a rule-or-ruin policy, and under the Roman governor, Felix, who was one of the most corrupt men ever to sit on that throne. Famine had impoverished the area (Acts 11:27ff.) and the poor were sore oppressed. The rich got richer and the poor got poorer. Keep these facts in mind.

Now let us go back to verse 1: Note that James calls himself simply "a servant of God and the Lord Jesus Christ." Is it not interesting that he does not identify himself as Jesus' half-brother? Perhaps it was because everyone knew him anyway, perhaps it was because of modesty, and perhaps it was because of what Jesus had said earlier: "For whosoever shall do the will of God, *the same* is my brother. . . ." (Mark 3:35ff.; emphasis mine). As George Bailey has said, "It is more important to be Christ's brother *in the faith* than *in the flesh.*"

Note also that James does not refer to his esteemed position at Jerusalem, but rather refers to himself as "a *servant* of God and of the Lord Jesus Christ." The word translated "servant" is *doulos*—bondservant or slave. James says, "I'm just a *slave* of Jesus."

## B. TO WHOM WRITTEN.

The second part of verse 1 has to do with those to whom the book is written. The book of James comes under the general classification of a "*general* epistle (or letter)"—"general" because it is not written by Paul and "general" because it is not addressed to a specific congregation or individual. It is rather addressed "to the twelve tribes which are scattered abroad."

The phrase "twelve tribes" is used by Paul to refer to the Jewish people as a whole (Acts 26:6, 7). The reading audience is further identified as "the twelve tribes *which are scattered abroad.*" Through the years, the Jews had been scattered by the Assyrians, by the Babylonians, and by conquering nations between the Testaments. Others had migrated to other locales on their own. But the question is: How is this phrasing used?

It seems obvious that James is *not* writing to all Jews everywhere, believers and unbelievers alike. Fifteen times he refers to his readers as "brethren" and these were "brethren" who had "the faith of our Lord Jesus Christ" (James 2:1). Some feel that the term refers to all Christians (Galatians 3:29). My personal opinion is that James is writing to *Christian Jews.*

But it really makes little difference, for the Holy Spirit preserved this book *for all of us.* Many of the New Testament writers slanted their writings to one group or another (under the guidance of the Spirit), but those writings were preserved under God's providence because they were applicable to all men in all ages. So regardless of the specific ones addressed, James wrote this because he wants US to be happy.

## C. THE SALUTATION: "GREETING."

The word "greeting" is translated from the root word for "rejoice." It means "to rejoice, to be HAPPY." It could be used just as a standard salutation without any particular meaning, but I believe James *meant* exactly what he said. He picks up the theme of happiness in the very next verse: "My brethren, count it all JOY. . . .";

This will probably be a good time to ask, "What is the overall PURPOSE of the book?"

Since James covers many topics in a short space, one must of necessity use some *general* phrase to cover the whole. One writer called the book "the Gospel of Common Sense." Again, an outline of the book can be centered around the topic of *faith*. In our lessons I will be identifying the purpose of the book as "PRACTICAL CHRISTIANITY."

The question being asked by all men concerning the religion of Christ is, "Does it really *work?*" James answers the question effectively, demonstrating the truth that the religion of Jesus is applicable in any age, in any situation! James gets down where we live!

To illustrate both the practicality of the book and the fact that James *does* want us to be happy, let's spend the last part of the lesson studying the next few verses.

## II. JAMES WANTS US TO BE HAPPY EVEN WHEN TROUBLES COME.
## Verses 2-4.

It is not hard to be happy when things are going well— when we have good health, plenty of money, good friends, success, the praise of men, security. The real challenge comes when the roof falls in—when we lose our health, when we're broke, when our friends desert us, when we're failures, when we're criticized, when there's no hope for the future!

Christian Jews knew that challenge. They had all the problems that all humans have *plus* the persecution that came to the Jews *plus* the persecution that came to Christians! But note what James says: "My brethren, count it all *joy* when ye fall into diverse [or various] temptations." (Emphasis mine.) The word translated "temptation" can refer to inward temptation or outward trials.

Note that they "fell into" these problems. They didn't "walk into" them. They didn't seek them out nor were these problems which came as a result of their failure to live right or to prepare for the future. These were troubles that came *in spite of* their best efforts to avoid trouble.

But when these trials *did* come, James said *this* should be their attitude: "Count it all *joy*." In other words, be happy; look on the bright side!

But *why* have a good attitude when problems arise? In the first few verses, the reason given is this: If we have the right attitude, problems will *develop our character*. "Knowing this that the trying of your faith worketh patience" (verse 3).

The word "trying" means "testing." Notice that it is our *faith* that is tested. If a person has faith when problems come, that person will be made stronger. If a person doesn't have faith, then problems in his life will make him weaker.

If one has faith, trials in his life will produce *patience*. The Greek word translated "patience" refers to "endurance, steadfastness." To the Jews, who had to endure so much through the years, this was the queen of virtues.

Whether we like it or not, that which makes us *stronger* is successfully meeting the challenges of life—and, yes, even to *suffer*. The coach that puts his team through a grueling schedule is not being mean; he is trying to make the team strong for the contests ahead.

Verse 4 says that we have every reason to be happy when problems come because the end result can be *maturity* in our lives: "But let patience have her perfect work, that ye may be perfect and entire, wanting [or lacking] nothing." "Let patience have her perfect work" means to *continue* to endure so that the end result or finished work of patient endurance can be seen. And what is that finished or perfect work? "That ye may be perfect and entire, wanting [or lacking] nothing." This does not refer to sinless perfection (James 3:2) but rather refers to spiritual *growth*. J. B. Phillips puts it this way: "And you will find you have become men of mature character, men of integrity with no weak spots."

When we put it all together, we have James telling us that if we keep on keeping-on regardless of the trials we confront, the end result will be that we will be even *better* able to meet the challenges of the *future*.

Like it or not, facing troubles with the help of God is the primary way that we grow up!!

## FOR DISCUSSION

1. Discuss the possible authors of the book. Why do most conservative scholars feel that "the Lord's brother" was the author?
2. Since Jesus and James were raised together, think of what you know about Jesus' early life (the synagogue school, visits to Jerusalem, the carpenter shop) and discuss what the early life of James might have been like.
3. Some claim James is a *Jewish* book. How many of the fifteen direct and indirect references to Jesus can you find in the book of James?
4. Note the many parallels between the teachings of Jesus and the writings of James. For instance these from the Sermon on the Mount:
   Matt. 5:1ff.   —James 1:2   Matt. 7:1      —James 4:11, 12
   Matt. 5:34-37—James 5:12   Matt. 7:7      —James 1:5
   Matt. 5:48     —James 1:4   Matt. 7:24-26—James 1:22
5. In some religions today "the ten lost tribes of Israel" figure prominently in their theology. Does verse 1 throw any light on this (see also II Chronicles 11:16, 17; Ezra 6:17)?

6. Do you think James was writing originally to all Christians or to Christian Jews? Why do you think that?
7. What should be the Christian's attitude toward trials (see also Matthew 5:10-12; Romans 5:3-5).
8. Glance through the book of James and list some of the trials James' readers had to undergo (James 2:6, 7; 5:1ff.; 5:6, 5:13ff.; etc.)
9. As a class you may wish to discuss some projects whereby your faith can work.

# THE PROVING GROUND
# OF OUR FAITH

*James 1:5-18*

James is the book that gets right down where we live. One individual said that every-time he read the book of James, he had the uneasy feeling that James had been reading his mail. The practicality of the book is seen in the very first topic it tackles: Trials and temptations and how they affect us. If there is anything universal to mankind, it is the fact that we all have problems.

What should be our reaction to the troubles and trials of life? In our last lesson, we noted that James said that we can be *happy* even when troubles come our way (James 1:2). The reason, James explained, is because if we meet the challenges of life with *faith*, they can help to develop our character (James 1:3, 4).

But James has *more* to say about problems and trials in verses 5 through 18—and that is our study for today.

The section *begins* by noting the need for *wisdom*: "If any of you lack wisdom. . . ." (James 1:5a). Wisdom is often contrasted with knowledge by noting that knowledge is primarily concerned with *facts* while wisdom is primarily concerned with the *application* of those facts. But let's go deeper into the meaning of this word. What would the word "wisdom" have meant to James' Jewish readers? The word most associated with wisdom in the Old Testament is the word "*understanding*." In the book of Proverbs wisdom and understanding are constantly linked, and often used interchangeably (Proverbs 1:2, 5; 4:7; etc.).

By "understanding," I do not mean understanding how to replace a faucet or understanding why birds fly south in the fall. Rather I mean, coming to understand things as God understands things, coming to see things as God sees them. The phrase *divine insight* well expresses it.

James is challenging us to rise above our problems and to see them in the proper perspective—to gain an *understanding* of trials and tribulations that will enable us to take whatever life may bring.


# I. WE NEED TO UNDERSTAND THAT GOD IS ALWAYS READY AND WILLING TO HELP US.
## Verses 5-8.

As already noted, verse 5 begins, "If any of you lack wisdom, let him ask of God. . . ." All of us feel the need for wisdom: Preachers, leaders of the church, Bible class teachers, parents, personal workers, *all* Christians. James says when you feel that need, go to God in prayer.

But in the immediate context, James is talking about the need for wisdom when *problems* come. He has said that you should "count it all joy" when you fall into trouble. You may have a hard time understanding that. If so, James says, Go to God; *He* will help you understand.

When problems come, we need to utilize *every* resource at our disposal. We can gain divine insight from a variety of sources—all provided by God. We can gain this from the Bible (Proverbs 1:2; II Timothy 3:15). We can also gain divine insight from those who are themselves wise in God's sight (Proverbs 10:31). And experience, as we strive to live as God wants us to live, can teach us much. *But* is it not true that all of us at some point of our lives have come to that point where we have apparently exhausted our resources? Where we are at our wits' end? When the secondary sources of divine insight fail to satisfy, we can go to the primary source of the wisdom: God Himself!

But what confidence can we have that God will answer our prayer for wisdom? James assures us if a man asks of God, God "giveth to all men liberally and upbraideth not; and it shall be given him" (James 1:5).

God "gives to all men." He doesn't play favorites among His children. "He gives to all men liberally." He is not stingy in His giving. And "he upbraideth not." God doesn't spoil His gifts by reproaching us for our need for them. Unlike some of us, God is a gracious giver.

Because of James' confidence in "the giving God," he says: "And it shall be given him"—one of the great Biblical affirmations of the power of prayer.

But James quickly adds that the prayer must be prayed in the right way. Throughout the New Testament, various conditions are noted for effective prayer. In this passage, James stresses the necessity of faith: "But let him ask in faith, nothing wavering. For he that wavereth is like a wave of the sea driven with the wind and tossed. For let not that man think that he shall receive anything of the Lord. A double-minded man is unstable in all his ways" (James 1:6-8).

"Double-minded" doesn't mean twice as smart. It refers to those of us who sometimes have a mind of faith and sometimes have a mind of doubt. Sometimes we think that God will answer our prayers and sometimes we think He won't. James uses the tossing of the sea to illustrate those of us who one moment are up in hope and the next moment are down in despair.

The word "unstable" is used to describe the doubter. This was the word used to describe the staggering of the drunk. If we put all the images of James together, we have the picture of a drunk man trying to keep his feet on the deck of a storm-tossed ship! I cannot imagine a picture of greater misery or uselessness!

Don't be filled with doubt, says James. *Believe*. Believe in a giving God to whom you can go in greatest confidence when troubles come your way!


## II. WE NEED TO UNDERSTAND THAT IT IS NOT OUTWARD CONDITIONS THAT MAKE US HAPPY OR SAD, BUT OUR INWARD RESPONSE.
### Verses 9-11.

James comes now to one of the most common problems of his day—and *any* day: The problem of *money*, having too little of it or too much of it.

In those days, most people were either very poor or very rich. *Either* condition has its special challenges.

The poor have a trial of body (they are exhausted), a trial of mind (it is hard to get an education), a trial of heart (it may be hard to give), a trial of temper (patience often wears thin). And the rich have their problems: Becoming distracted from the really important things in life, special cares and responsibilities, the danger of feeling self-sufficient.

But as great as these challenges were (and are), James says that *whatever* your financial situation, you can *still* be happy: "Let the brother of low degree rejoice in that he is exalted. But the rich in that he is made low" (James 1:9, 10a).

James first speaks to "the brother of low degree" and tells him to learn *self-respect*.

The brother of low degree was the poor man, humbled by circumstances. Today we use expressions like "low man on the totem pole." This is the sort of situation we *gripe* about, but James says, "Rejoice." Why? Because the poor man who is a Christian is actually "exalted." From the standpoint of the world he is on the bottom rung of the ladder; from the standpoint of the things that count, he is on the top rung. He may not have all the gadgets the next man has, but he is "rich" (Revelation 2:9; Philippians 4:19). When your Father owns *everything*, you can hold your head up high.

But James also speaks to "the rich [brother]" and gives him divine insight into handling *his* special challenge. He can rejoice, says James, "in that he is made low." The rich can be happy if they learn *self-abasement.*

The rich Christian striving to do the will of God is "brought low" in at least two ways: In his own estimation and in service. He also learned the transient nature of the *things* that make him rich—so constantly under attack by moth, rust, and thieves (Matthew 6:19, 20). (And today, we'd have to add "inflation"!)

But further, he is aware of the transient nature of life itself! "As the flower of the grass he shall pass away. For the sun is no sooner risen with a burning heat, but it withereth the grass, and the flower thereof falleth, and grace of the fashion of it perisheth: so also shall the rich man fade away in his ways" (James 1:10b, 11).

Christianity has been called "the great equalizer." It elevates the poor man in his humble estate. It humbles the rich man in his elevated estate. How fortunate is the man who has learned what Paul learned: "I have learned in *whatsoever* state I am, therewith to be content" (Philippians 4:11; emphasis mine). It is not the outward circumstances of life that make us happy or sad, but rather our response, our *attitude.* If we would be happy, there is no more important bit of divine insight than this!

### III. WE NEED TO UNDERSTAND THAT PROBLEMS ARE THE "PROVING GROUND" FOR OUR FAITH.
### Verse 12.

In verse 12, James returns to the general attitude a Christian should have when problems come. He said earlier that a Christian should "count it all joy" when he has problems because those problems could result in character growth. Now he tells us another value of trials: "Blessed [happy] is the man that endureth temptation: for when he is tried, he shall receive the crown of life, which the Lord hath promised to them that love him" (James 1:12).

The word "tried" signifies one who has been tried or tested and who has *met* the test. The ASV has "approved." The idea is *tried-and-true*.

Most of us are familiar with testing laboratories or proving grounds. Whether it be shatterproof bottles or the latest automobile, new products go through grueling tests to assure that they will perform as they should. When they *pass* the test, they are *approved*. If the tests have been adequate, we use that product with confidence.

Even so, says James, this world with all its problems is the proving ground for our faith. If we have had no problems, we have an untested faith; we do not know whether it will hold up under real burdens or not. But if with the help of God, we have stood the worst that life can bring, we can go forth into the world with confidence. That Christian *can* be happy who has "endured temptation" and has come out with his faith intact.

But there is more to the "proving ground" than this. The manufacturer watches nervously while his product is in testing and then *rejoices* when the product is approved, for now he has a good chance to make a profit. If *we* meet the test of life, we have much more than a monetary reward to look forward to. When we have passed the *last* test, then we have God's "seal of approval" and *heaven* is our reward: "He shall receive the crown of life, which the Lord hath promised to them that love him" (James 1:12c). Surely such a prospect can help us over some very rough moments!

# IV. WE NEED TO UNDERSTAND THE NEED FOR ACCEPTING *PERSONAL RESPONSIBILITY* FOR OUR SIN.
## Verses 13-18.

The last piece of divine insight that James gives us in this discussion of trials has to do with the real *source* of temptation. To me the main thrust of verses 13 through 18 is the need for each individual to accept *personal responsibility* for his own sin.

James has said so much about the *value* of trials and problems that some might have gotten the idea that God personally and deliberately sends us all our problems so that we can receive the benefits. So James quickly says: "Let no man say when he is tempted, I am tempted by God...." (James 1:13a).

In the previous verses, the emphasis has been on the outward problems and trials of life; in verses 12 through 18, however, that which we usually refer to as "temptation" is in view: "Let no man say when he is tempted [to do wrong], I am tempted of God [to do that wrong]...."

From the beginning, men have played "the blame game." They have wanted to blame *others* (including God) for their own failures: "The woman whom *thou* gavest to be with me, *she* gave me of the tree, and I did eat" (Genesis 3:12; emphasis mine). Today we want to blame environment— or heredity—or God—or anybody or anything other than *ourselves* for all our problems. "I couldn't help myself. After all God made me quick-tempered"—or whatever.

James says, Stop blaming God! "Let no man say when he is tempted, I am tempted of God: for God cannot be tempted with evil, neither tempteth he any man" (James 1:13). God does not set up some kind of cosmic "Sting," to try to trap or ensnare us. By His very nature, He neither sins nor encourages us to sin.

If God is not the source of our temptation, what is? "But every man is tempted, when he is drawn away of *his own lust,*

25

and enticed" (James 1:14; emphasis mine).

Satan is the Tempter (Matthew 4:4; I Thessalonians 3:5), but that which enables him to tempt us is *our own* weaknesses. The RSV reads, "Each person is tempted when he is lured and enticed by *his own* desire."

Satan is aware of our weaknesses and he uses these most effectively in luring us away from God. The words translated "drawn away" and "enticed" were originally used to describe the art of the fisher and hunter. James is saying that *we* supply the bait that Satan uses to hook us and to trap us! Satan can't "make us" do anything that we don't *want* to do.

Elsewhere in the New Testament, it is stressed that we do *not* have to give in to our lusts (Romans 8:13; James 4:7). But what if we are self-indulgent? What if we give free rein to our baser passions? What if we say, "I just can't help myself"? James says this is the result: "Then when lust hath conceived, it bringeth forth sin: and sin when it is finished, bringeth forth *death* (James 1:15; emphasis mine).

It is very important that we grasp the consequences of the self-indulgent, irresponsible life. I want you to see the full picture James paints for us here. He is very graphic.

The words "drawn away" and "enticed" (verse 14) were originally used to describe the angler or hunter. But they came to refer to the allurement of the prostitute. James personifies lust, our own lust, as that prostitute, trying to get us to sin. When we *give in* to our unlawful desire, whatever it might be, there is conception—and at last *sin* is born. Sin, the child of our *own* folly.

But the picture is still not finished. I do not have to let sin live. By repentance, confession, turning back to God, that "child" can be banished. *But* on the other hand, I can nourish that child. I can refuse to repent. I can try to justify myself for what I did. I can watch that child grow. And *then* that child is "finished" or full-grown (ASV), it will in time bring forth a child, a grotesque monster with a grinning skull head, my spiritual grandchild—*spiritual death* (verse

15)—and I am doomed.

So James says, "Do not err, my beloved brethren" (James 1:16). "Do not err" in accusing God of being responsible for your sin. Accept the responsibility *yourself*.

God is only capable of giving good gifts: "Every good gift and every perfect gift is from above, and cometh down from the Father of lights, with whom is no variableness, neither shadow or turning" (James 1:17).

The light from the sun, the moon, the stars may vary, but God does not. Only good comes from Him! As proof James gives one final illustration: God is the source of the greatest gift of all, our salvation: "Of his own will begat he us [literally, he brought us forth] with the word of truth, that we should be a kind of firstfruits of his creatures" (James 1:18).

If I am to be one of God's spiritual "firstfruits," I must learn *personal responsibility*. I must stay away from temptation. I must learn to not entertain improper desires. And I must learn to confess my sin and return to the Lord when I fail! But if I will do *my* part, God will be with me and I *can* be victorious over the trials and temptations of life!

## FOR DISCUSSION

1. What are some problems common to all mankind? What are some special problems related to being a *Christian*?
2. Discuss the phrase "upbraideth not" (James 1:5). Did the Lord "upbraid" James after His resurrection?
3. Does it pay to pray today (James 1:5)?
4. How can we develop more faith, so our prayers will be helped (James 1:6)?
5. What are some of the other conditions of acceptable prayer?
6. Guy N. Woods notes that some think doubt is an "evidence of superior learning or unusual intellectual attainment." What does James say about this (James 1:6-8)?
7. Discuss Christianity as "the great equalizer" (James 1:9-11).

8. Discuss Agur's prayer in Proverbs 30:8, 9.
9. What are some of the things on which people place the blame for their sin?
10. See if you can find the progression of lust, sin, and death (James 1:15) in Joshua 7:21, 25.
11. Discuss the meaning of the terms "variableness," "shadow of turning," and "firstfruits" in verses 17 and 18.

# HOW'S YOUR RECEPTION?

*James 1:19-27*

In the physical world most of us recognize the importance of good reception. When I have to travel in the car, I enjoy the radio during the day. But when evening comes and the airways are bombarded with the super-station signals from Mexico and elsewhere, all spilling over into a dozen other bands, it becomes impossible to receive a single station for any period of time. Trying to listen is a headache.

But reception of a radio program amounts to nothing compared with the reception of *God's word.* The question of this passage is, what is your *attitude* toward that word? How is your *spiritual* reception?

## I. WE MUST BE READY TO
## RECEIVE THE WORD.
## Verses 19-21.

James begins by saying that if we are to have receptive hearts, several things must characterize us: "Wherefore, my beloved brethren, let every man be swift to hear, slow to speak, slow to wrath: For the wrath of man worketh not the righteousness of God" (James 1:19, 20).

We are to be "swift to hear, slow to speak, slow to

wrath." Unfortunately most of us are slow to hear, swift to speak, and swift to wrath! In context each characteristic ties in with our reception of God's word:

"Swift to hear." At least two things are involved here: (1) an eagerness to learn, and (2) a willingness to accept. The person with this quality takes advantage of every opportunity to learn and listens with rapt attention, ready to obey. There's an art to good listening! Great listeners make great preaching.

"Slow to speak." This does not refer to slowness *when* speaking, but being slow to *start* speaking. This is good general advice: "In the multitude of words there wanteth not [or lacketh not] sin: But he that refraineth his lips is wise" (Proverbs 10:19). But this refers in a special way to the reception of God's word. It is almost impossible to learn while you are talking. Wilson Myner said, "A good listener is not only popular everywhere, but after awhile he knows something."

Finally, "slow to wrath." Again this is good general advice. Verse 20 stresses that "the wrath of man worketh not the righteousness of God." Or as the NIV translates the verse: "Man's anger does not bring about the righteous life that God desires." But in context, the words "slow to wrath" are primarily concerned about the reception of God's word. I have known people who left congregations because they didn't like the preaching on worldliness, divorce, and the like.

When God's word hits you, the conscience begins to smart. There are at least two ways that you can soothe that conscience: You can repent, change your life, receive forgiveness, and thus have peace of mind. Or you can become angry and attack the one who brought the unpleasant truth, thus turning attention from yourself to another and thus easing your conscience. But let it be clearly understood that the latter course is spiritual suicide!

But how can we have the kind of mind that is receptive, "swift to hear, slow to speak, [and] slow to wrath"? The answer is *preparation*. In verse 21, James uses the illustration of preparing the garden to receive the seed: "Wherefore lay apart all filthiness and superfluity of naughtiness, and receive with meekness the engrafted word, which is able to save your souls." Moffatt translates the first part of the verse, "So clear away all the foul rank growth." In physical gardening, we recognize the need to get rid of the bad to give the good the best possible chance—and this is also true in the spiritual realm.

We need to eradicate every spiritual trait contrary to God's will, but James mentions two especially noxious "weeds" that *have* to go if we are to receive God's word: "Filthiness and superfluity of naughtiness." "Filthiness" is commonly used in the scriptures to refer to that which is filthy or repulsive (Zechariah 3:3, 4). Used in a general way it refers to moral uncleanness. "Superfluity of naughtiness" is translated "overflowing of wickedness" in the ASV. Imagine obnoxious and persistent weeds spreading quickly over all the land that you are trying to cultivate.

We need to recognize the *loathsomeness* of sin. As long as sin is attractive to us, we will never be in a position to accept truth. But when sin is *repulsive* to us, then we can follow James' instruction at the last of the verse: "Receive with meekness the engrafted word, which is able to save your souls."

Meekness is not weakness; it is rather inward strength voluntarily submitting to the will of God. In that kind of receptive "soil," the seed of God's word (Luke 8:11) can do great things. In an effort to convey the full concept of the word "engrafted," some translations have the words "planted" or "implanted" or even "rooted." The picture is of the plant growing down, becoming firmly rooted and fixed in the soil, and thus becoming strong and healthy. When *God's word* becomes thus "rooted and fixed" in our hearts and minds, we can have great hope for the future.

Properly received, God's word is a *powerful* thing. The last part of verse 21 is a great tribute to that power: "The engrafted word, *which is able* to save your souls." The phrase "which is able" is a form of the Greek word trans-lated "power" in Romans 1:16, the Greek word from which we get "dynamic, dynamo, *dynamite*." In Romans 1:16, God's word has power to save the unbeliever; in James 1:21, God's word has power to *continue* to save the child of God.


## II. WE MUST BE READY TO
## OBEY THE WORD.
### Verses 22-25.

But when *does* that powerful word save us? *Reception* of the word includes *obeying* that word. I can hardly be said to be "receptive" to my doctor's instructions if I fail to obey them. James says: "But be ye *doers* of the word, and not hearers only, deceiving your own selves" (James 1:22; emphasis mine).

The "hearers" in this verse are far different from those who are "swift to hear" (verse 19). These hearers are sermon-tasters with a lecture-attender mentality, whose *lives* are not affected by what they hear. It has always been far easier to fill our buildings with hearers than with doers. We have far too many homiletic hearers, sermon samplers, lecture listeners, evangelistic evaluators, didactic dissec-tors, and preacher puller-aparts, who do not *apply* the message to *themselves*, who "go away" unaffected. Such individuals, says James, are self-deceived.

Jesus compared this type of individual with a foolish man building his house on the shifting sand (Matthew 7:26, 27). James uses *this* illustration: "For if any be a hearer of the word, and not a doer, he is like unto a man beholding his natural face in a glass: For he beholdeth himself, and goeth his way, and straightway forgetteth what manner of man he was" (James 1:23, 24).

The illustration is that of looking at oneself in a mirror.

The phrase "natural face" refers to the one you're born with, the one other people have to look at. Sometimes I look at my "natural face"—when I look in the mirror, especially in the morning. There's my face, puffy with sleep and covered with a scruffy stubble. There's the bloodshot eyes, filled with sleep. And the tousled hair with the perennial cowlick.

That "natural face" doesn't do much for me, but as addled as I am when I first wake up, I still have enough common sense to know that depressing look in the mirror will do me no good unless I *do* something about what I see. So I repair the damage as best I can: I shave, I wash my face, I comb my hair. But if I were like the foolish man depicted in verse 24, I would look at myself and then go away, having done nothing about what I had seen, and even *forgetting* what I had seen.

I don't know *why* the foolish man did nothing about what he saw. Maybe he didn't recognize the reflected image as himself. Some of the primitive tribes in New Guinea have no mirrors. When visitors take pictures, the natives are able to recognize others in the pictures, but not themselves. Or maybe he did nothing about what he saw because he had some confused idea that the situation would correct itself "somehow," "some way."

Probably the best suggestion as to why he did nothing about it ties in with the phrase "he . . . goeth his way." He turned to other things and immediately became so involved that he forgot "what manner of man he was." It is not uncommon for people to hear God's truth and to be moved for the moment, but then they leave and are quickly caught up in the world again, and the moment is gone—sometimes forever. *Whatever* the reason, James indicates that it is foolish, ridiculous, pathetic, to *know* what needs to be done and not to do it.

In contrast to that, James then speaks of the man who looks into "the mirror" and *does something* about what he sees: "But whoso looketh into the perfect law of liberty, and continueth therein, he being not a forgetful hearer, but a doer of the work, this man shall be blessed in his deed" (James 1:25).

This verse tells us three things about God's word: It is a "law"—because it contains commands from our King Jesus. The New Testament is not a legal system as was the Old Testament, but it still contains "laws," basic principles which must guide our life (Galatians 6:2; Romans 3:27; 8:2). But it is not only a "law"; it is a "perfect law." "Perfect" is from *telos*, "last" or "end" or "complete." The New Testament is God's final revelation to earth dwellers, satisfying every spiritual need (II Timothy 3:16, 17). Finally, it is the "perfect law of *liberty*." The words "law" and "liberty" may appear to be contradictory, but real liberty and freedom come only when there are laws that protect our freedom. The only really *free* people spiritually are those who have voluntarily submitted themselves to the service of God because of their love and appreciation.

This "perfect law of liberty" is compared to a *mirror*. If I will take the time to look at myself in the mirror of God's word, comparing my life with its teachings, I will see myself—not necessarily as I would like to be, but *as I really am.*

But that look will not help me if I do nothing about it. Nor will it bless me if I stop looking and forget "what manner of man" I am. "But whoso looketh into the perfect law of liberty, and *continueth* therein, he being not a forgetful hearer, but a *doer* of the work, *this man* shall be blessed in his deed." There's no other way to have God's blessings!

### III. WE MUST BE READY
### TO *LIVE* THE WORD
### Verses 26, 27.

But what is the sort of thing involved in doing the word? In the next two verses, James gives three illustrations of being an attentive doer instead of a forgetful hearer, three examples of *practical* Christianity:

A. SPEAKING: "If any man among you seem to be religious, and bridleth not his tongue, but deceiveth his own heart, this man's religion is vain" (James 1:26). The words "religious" and "religion" come from a Greek word that refers to the *outward* manifestation of religion—external rites or services. So the man pictured goes to "the services." He sings, he prays and gives, he partakes of the Lord's Supper. But when he leaves, he has an "unbridled tongue." He uses vile language, he badmouths others, he praises himself, he fills the air with useless words.

Two things are true of him, says James: He is self-deceived like the fellow in verse 22—for he, too, is a hearer and not a doer. And his religion is "vain"—empty, useless. No man can get to heaven "on a vain religion"! He gets caught in his own mouthtrap.

B. SHARING: "Pure religion and undefiled before God and the Father is this, To visit the fatherless and widows in their affliction. . . ." (James 1:27a). In contrast with *vain*, empty, religion, James tells about "pure" and "undefiled" religion that meets God's approval.

On the positive side, James says that we are to help people. The English words "fatherless" and "widows" indicate those who have lost fathers or husbands by *death*, but the *Greek* words will allow wider usage. Death is not the only thing that can remove the breadwinner. There's also desertion, drink, disease, dope, divorce, and delinquency. These are people in *real* need, representative of all who have physical, spiritual, or emotional needs.

And what is the response of "pure religion" to these needs? The text has "visit." This word is not limited to a social call. The word infers "going to see *to take care of needs.*" Thus the NEB translates "visit" as "go to the help of." In some cases a friendly call *may* be what is needed, but many times there are other needs, some very pressing.

But there is also another side of this "pure religion":

35

C. SEPARATING: "Pure religion and undefiled before God and the Father is this, To visit the fatherless and widows in their affliction, *and to keep himself unspotted from the world*" (James 1:27; emphasis mine). James is speaking to today's generation. Many believe that just as long as your heart is good and you are generous, that your *lifestyle* is not all that important. But James tells every man "to keep himself unspotted from the world"!

What a challenge this is in today's world! A young man once stopped his newly-cleaned car in front of a house, walked up to the house, and asked if he could park there. The man of the house told him, "You can *park* your nice clean car here, but you can't *drive it away*." The young man thought it was a joke and left his car while he went about his business. He returned a few hours later to find his car covered with mud. He had parked by two mud holes and the passing traffic had done the rest. He did *not* drive a clean car away! The world today is *filled* with sin "mud holes." What a challenge to keep from getting spotted!

To stay "unspotted," we need to stay away from situations where sin abounds—stay away from "big" sins, "little" sins, the obviously sinful and even the questionable. And we need always to stay close to Jesus that our "robes" might be constantly "washed . . . white in the blood of the lamb" (Revelation 9:14). In short, we need to be *different* from the world!

If we are to live the word, we must have *both* the positive and negative in our lives. Once a high-society lady went with a social worker to the wrong side of the tracks to do "her bit" for charity. As they were departing, after leaving a supply of food, clothing, and other items, a ragged little urchin raced by them almost knocking the well-dressed woman down. The matron was repulsed and said to the social worker: "Why isn't he cleaned up? Doesn't his mother love him?!" The social worker replied: "Yes, his mother loves him. Some people love children, but don't hate dirt." And then she added: "And there are some people who hate dirt, but don't love children." May God help *us* to be the kind of people who have a *balanced* view of Christianity: Let us *love people* and *also hate spiritual "dirt."*

## FOR DISCUSSION

1. What are some things that will hinder the reception of the word?
2. Is James writing to Christians or non-Christians? Does this mean that Christians can have the same "reception" problems as nonmembers? Can you think of any examples?
3. Discuss "How to Be a Good Listener."
4. How can one overcome a "quick temper"? Discuss I Corinthians 9:27 and Philippians 4:13.
5. Which is to be more pitied—the one who is other-deceived or the one who is self-deceived (James 1:22)?
6. In what sense of the word is the New Testament a "law" (James 1:25)?
7. In addition to using a mirror to look into, it can be used in a periscope, to reflect sunlight, etc. Use this to illustrate the good and bad uses made of the Bible (James 1:25).
8. What are some ways we fail to "bridle" our tongues?
9. What is the church's responsibility for caring for the widows and orphans?
10. Discuss the word "visit" (James 1:27). What are some occasions when much more is needed than just a casual social visit?
11. DISCUSS SOME PRACTICAL WAYS THAT YOUR CLASS CAN HELP THE NEEDY—NOW.
12. Discuss the problem of *worldliness* in the church.

# IS YOUR HEART FILLED WITH PREJUDICE?

*James 2:1-13*

James begins: "My brethren, have not the faith of our Lord Jesus Christ, the Lord of glory, *with respect of persons*" (James 2:1; emphasis mine). The NASB has "My brethren, do not hold your faith . . . *with an attitude of personal favoritism.*" The NKJV has "with *partiality.*" "Respect of persons," "personal favoritism," "partiality"—such were common sins in James' day *and in ours.*

The *root* of these attitudes is *prejudice.* How easy it is to become prejudiced toward others—as individuals or as a class of people. A common giveaway of this kind of prejudice are the words "every" or "all": "All Jews are money-mad," "all politicians are crooked," "all preachers are long-winded," "all (fill in the blank) are morally lax." We make such statements glibly, not knowing how they hurt others, as we are surrounded by others who feel as we do. It is only when we become the target of such libel that the meanness and littleness of such attitudes come home.

To stress the SERIOUSNESS of prejudice, James makes appeal to four of the most basic and fundamental doctrines of the New Testament: The deity of Jesus. The sovereignty of God. The authority of God's word. And the certainty of judgment. It would be hard to imagine four more solemn and awesome topics. James turns the biggest of big guns on the sin of showing favoritism. Don't be a respecter of persons . . .

# I. BECAUSE THIS IS CONTRARY TO THE FAITH WE HAVE IN JESUS.
## Verses 1-4.

"My brethren," says James, "have not [or hold not] the faith of our Lord Jesus Christ, the Lord of glory, with respect of persons" (verse 1). "The faith of our Lord Jesus Christ" refers to the faith *we* have in Jesus. James says He is "Lord"—the Ruler of our lives. He is "Jesus"—our Savior. He is "Christ"—our anointed Prophet, Priest, and King. And He is "the Lord of *glory*." In the Old Testament, God's glory or Shekinah indicated the *presence* of God—as in the Tabernacle (Exodus 24:14; 40:34; Numbers 14:10). James is testifying to Jesus' *deity* (John 1:1cf.). James declares that if you really *believe* in Jesus as Lord, Christ, and God, it is *inconsistent* to show respect of persons.

But what does "respect of persons" mean? The phrase does not mean that we can never respect anyone (as we normally use the word "respect") nor that we cannot show honor to the deserving (Romans 13:7). The phrase "respect of persons" is translated from the Greek word for *face* plus the Greek word for *accept* or *receive*. It literally means to accept someone on the basis of his *face*, i.e., on the basis of superficial, outward appearance. The phrase thus referred to making a judgment concerning someone on a superficial basis and then *acting* toward that person as though that judgment were valid.

This type of prejudice and partiality is contrary to everything Jesus *was*. Jesus showed no respect of persons on the basis of occupation (Matthew 4:18, 19; 9:9). He showed no respect of persons on the basis of social standing (Matthew 9:10; Luke 7:36). He showed no respect of persons on the basis of race (John 4:9cf.; Matthew 8:5, 10). It is contrary to everything Jesus *taught*. For instance, John 7:24: "Stop judging by mere appearances" (NIV). It is contrary to everything Jesus *stood for*. He loved *all*. He died for all. James is saying to us that we need to look at people through the eyes of *Jesus*.

James then gives a concrete example of the type of thing he has in mind: "For if there come unto your assembly a man with a gold ring, in goodly apparel, and there come in also a poor man in vile raiment; and ye have respect to him that weareth the gay clothing, and say unto him, Sit thou here in a good place; and say to the poor, Stand thou there, or sit here under my footstool: Are ye not then partial in yourselves, and are become judges of [or with] evil thoughts?" (James 2:2-4).

The scene is that of a worship service in the first century. Their assemblies were public and open. One comes in wearing what the KJV calls "gay clothing." The literal meaning is "splendid clothing." This man is *rich*. The original says that he was "gold-ringed." He had one or more rings on many of his fingers. The literal meaning of "goodly" apparel is "bright or shining" apparel. This man *glittered* as he walked!

In contrast, James said, "And there come in also a poor man in vile raiment." In those days, "poor" did not mean "short of ready cash." It signified those in desperate financial condition, those with nothing but the clothes on their backs. In this case, the clothes on the poor man's back were no asset. The Greek word is from the same root as the word translated "filthiness" in James 1:21. The clothing was in bad shape and probably retained the pungent odor of tears, sweat, and despair.

Presumably both men were strangers, for there seems to have been no knowledge of the men's character. All judgment was made strictly on the basis of outward appearance. And the result?: "Ye have respect to him that weareth the gay [or splendid] clothing, and say unto him, Sit thou here in a good place; and say to the poor, Stand thou there, or sit here under my footstool" (verse 3).

The "usher" takes a look at the man in the rich finery and finds him the best seat in the house. But to the poor man he says, "You can stand at the back or can sit on the floor." Cash was more important than character.

I don't know why that poor man came. If he came to find help and concern, how disappointed he must have been! Instead of a rescue station for the lost, he found a haven for the stately pious. If he came seeking salvation, I'm sure he never came back again.

Listen to James' condemnation: "Are ye not then partial in yourselves, and are become judges of evil thoughts?" (verse 4). "Of evil thoughts" is a descriptive phrase. A good translation would be, "You have become evil-thinking judges." To make superficial judgments concerning others, colored by our prejudices, is *evil*.

## II. BECAUSE IT IS CONTRARY TO THE WILL OF GOD.
### Verses 5-7.

James begins the next section: "Hearken, my beloved brethren, Hath not God chosen the poor of this world rich in faith, and heirs of the kingdom which he hath promised to them that love him? But ye have despised the poor" (James 2:5, 6a).

God is "no respecter of persons" (Acts 10:34, 35). National differences are no longer important to Him (Acts 10:34). Social differences are unimportant to Him (Ephesians 6:9). In fact, James says, God has "chosen the poor of this world rich in faith and heirs of the kingdom."

This does not mean that God gave preferential treatment to the poor over the rich. "Chosen" is used in the common New Testament sense of referring to those who had *responded* to God's invitation. God "chose" the poor because it was the poor who came to the Lord and did His will. It was said concerning Jesus, "The *common* people heard him gladly" (Mark 12:37; emphasis mine).

In contrast to this, James says, "But *ye* have despised the poor." They had despised or dishonored the poor man by making him stand while they gave the rich man the choice seat. It is possible that they embraced the common philosophy that riches were a proof within themselves of God's approval in a special way. But this is not true, says James. The poor might be deficient in this world's goods, but they were "rich in faith, and heirs of the kingdom."

Actually, James continues, your practice of preferring the rich over the poor makes no sense at all—for you are honoring the very ones who make your life the most miserable. "Do not rich men oppress you, and draw you before the judgment seats? Do not they blaspheme that worthy name by the which ye are called?" (James 2:6b, 7).

The rich referred to here would have been non-Christians. Two specific types of oppression are mentioned by James:

(1) They used their influence in the corrupt courts of the day. To "draw . . . before the judgment seats" referred to bringing the defenseless man to trial against his will (we still speak of being "dragged" or "hauled" into court). The poor man didn't stand a chance.

(2) They blasphemed "that worthy name" by which they were called. "That worthy name" was the name of Christ. In the original, "by the which ye are called," literally reads "which was called upon you." The name of Christ was "called upon them" when they were baptized (Acts 2:38). Rich nonbelievers blasphemed, made light of, slandered the holy name of Christ.

How *foolish* then, James is saying, to give preferential treatment to the rich over the poor. As Calvin put it: "Why should a man honor his executioners and at the same time injure his friends?"

# III. BECAUSE IT IS CONTRARY TO THE AUTHORITATIVE WORD.
## Verses 8-11.

God not only practices nondiscrimination, He tells *us* to do the same. "If ye fulfill the royal law according to the scripture, Thou shalt love thy neighbor as thyself, ye do well: But if ye have respect of persons, ye commit sin, and are convinced [or convicted] of the law as transgressors" (James 2:8, 9).

Search the Bible through and you'll never find these exact words: "Do not discriminate against others because of their social standing, or their background, or their color." What you *will* find are *principles* that teach us we should not thus behave. One of the most important of these principles is found in the words, "Thou shalt love thy neighbor as thyself." This was first given in the Old Testament (Leviticus 19:18). Jesus echoed this basic truth and made it part of His covenant (Matthew 22; Mark 12; Luke 10).

Loving one's neighbor is called "the royal law." It may be called that because of its exalted position among the King's edicts. Or it may be called that because it is to be followed by those of us who are a *royal* priesthood (I Peter 2:9). *Whatever* the reason, James stresses its importance. Those who fulfill this law "do well."

But on the other hand if you do not love all men but rather "have respect of persons, ye commit sin, and are convinced [convicted] of the law as transgressors" (verse 9). He has told them that prejudice is inconsistent, a mistake, even foolish. But now he tells them plainly that it is a *sin*, a transgression of God's will. To them, it may have been relatively unimportant but James wants them to know that those who are guilty violate God's word!

James hammers this point home with these sobering words: "For whosoever shall keep the whole law, and yet offend in one point, he is guilty of all. For he that said, Do not commit adultery, said also, Do not kill. Now if thou commit no adultery, yet if thou kill, thou art become a transgressor of the law" (James 2:10, 11).

What James says may sound hard to you. "Offend in one point" means to "disobey one point of the law." If you do that, says James, you become "guilty of all." We should note that James is *not* saying that if you commit one sin, you might as well give up. Nor is he saying that if you commit one sin, you might as well go ahead and commit them all. What he *is* saying is that we cannot think of some sins as big and important and others as little and unimportant. James wants us to know that sin is sin and the committing of any sin makes us a sinner, the breaking of any law makes us a lawbreaker.

Many comparisons have been drawn to illustrate this truth. Dwight L. Moody pictured a man suspended over a chasm, held up by a chain. He noted that only *one* link had to break to hurl that man downward. Others have noted that if you get stopped for speeding, it will do no good to protest that you have killed no one; you will still be penalized for being a lawbreaker. But James' own illustration cannot be improved upon: "He that said, Do not commit adultery, said also, Do not kill. Now if thou commit no adultery, yet if thou kill, thou art become a transgressor of the law" (verse 11). The two commands given here have always been part of God's will for man. It is not, however, necessary to break them *both* to be a lawbreaker. Break only *one* and you are a lawbreaker in God's sight.

Thus one cannot say, "So what if my heart is filled with prejudice? I am not a murderer or an adulterer, so therefore I am really a fine person." No, says James, when you show respect of persons, you have disobeyed God. You have become a lawbreaker. You have become "guilty of all." Realizing this should drive each of us to our knees in penitence and prayer and make us resolve to remove prejudice from our hearts!

# IV. BECAUSE JUDGMENT IS SURE.
## Verses 12, 13.

Judgment is sure (Hebrews 9:27). In light of this, "So speak ye and so do, as they that shall be judged by the law of liberty" (James 2:12). In this verse, the instructions are directly related to the sin of discrimination:

(1) "Speaking" was part of their sin. They *said* to the rich man, "Sit thou here in a good place" and they *said* to the poor man, "Stand thou there, or sit here under my footstool." So often it is in our *words* that the prejudices in our hearts are exposed. Our words to and about others can show concern and compassion or our words can be filled with criticism and bitterness.

(2) And "doing" was part of their sin—as they ushered the rich and the poor to their respective seats. Ultimately our prejudices cause us to treat men differently. If we love all, our *lives* will show it.

Why be concerned about our "speaking" and "doing"? Because we will all be "judged by the law of liberty." James uses the same term as he did in James 1:25; the "law of liberty" refers to the New Testament of Jesus Christ. In light of this judgment (John 12:48; Romans 2:16), we need to put forth every effort to remove prejudice from our hearts! Listen to the first part of verse 13: "For he shall have judgment without mercy, that hath showed no mercy."

But all of us have failed to some extent. Is there therefore no hope at all? As if to answer this question, James closes on this encouraging note: "And mercy rejoiceth against judgment" (James 2:13b).

"Rejoiceth against" is translated in one version as "triumphs over," in another as "exalts over." In today's idiom, we might say, "Mercy *laughs in the face of* judgment." Because of God's mercy we need not fear the judgment. God's mercy makes up what I lack, assuming that I am truly diligent (Hebrews 11:6) in doing His will. James is saying that, all other things being equal, the man who shows mercy is the man who will receive mercy—and thus can rejoice when he thinks about the coming judgment!

I do not know of any more terrifying phrase than this: "Judgment without mercy"! Judgment without mercy means certain condemnation! All of us are sinners (Romans 3:23); without mercy we are lost. But this is what one has to look forward to if he does not have mercy, love, concern for all men!

# FOR DISCUSSION

1. Check a variety of translations to see how the phrase "respect of persons" is translated in the different ones.
2. Discuss prejudice in general. *Is* this a sin that most people don't consider very serious?
3. Have you ever been on the receiving end of prejudice? Share an experience or two. Did you enjoy being classed together with a particular group—or do you prefer being treated as an individual, accepted or rejected on your own merits?
4. One expression of prejudice is cliquishness. What is the difference between "a clique" and "a group of close friends"?
5. The word "assembly" (James 2:2) is literally "synagogue." Why would James have used such a term?
6. Think about the rich man's apparel (James 2:2-4). Should our assemblies be used for fashion parades?
7. Discuss the work of an "usher" (James 2:3).
8. Would *you* have wanted the poor man to sit next to you?
9. Why are the poor often more responsive than the rich?
10. Do some of us go to the opposite extreme from our text and show preferential treatment to the poor over the rich? Is either extreme right?
11. Is it easy to love everybody—when they may differ from us in race, color, or background? How can we develop more love for all men?

# IS YOUR FAITH ALIVE
# AND WELL?

*James 2:14-26*

Do you like controversy? Or rather do you break out in hives when there is disagreement? If you do, you may want to rub on a generous amount of your favorite ointment before we begin our study of James 2:14-26. This probably is the section of James that caused Luther to call the book an epistle of straw. This is the section of the book that elicits the strongest strugglings among commentators.

But why all this consternation? Because in this passage, James says that faith without works *is useless*, faith without works *cannot be demonstrated*, faith without works *cannot change a person*, faith without works *is not perfected*, and faith without works *is dead!* And this will not do if you've decided from isolated passages from the pen of Paul that works, *any* kind of works, have nothing whatever to do with our salvation!

But lest you become discouraged about our present study, let me quickly suggest that there is nothing in James that contradicts Paul. Paul stresses that we are not saved *on the basis of* our works (Romans 4:1-5), but he never discounts the necessity of *obedience* (Romans 1:1, 5; 16:26). On the other hand, James constantly stresses the importance of faith, but he wants us to know that the faith that saves is the faith that *obeys*.

It will be my purpose in this presentation to emphasize both faith *and* works—to show the necessity of both. I'll be asking these questions: "Is *your* faith alive and well?" and "Is *my* faith alive and well?"

## I. FAITH WITHOUT WORKS IS USELESS.
### Verses 14-17.

James begins by asking the question: "What doth it profit my brethren, though a man say he hath faith, and have not works? Can faith save him?" (James 2:14). Of what *value* is saying one has faith if one does not work, does not obey? The NEB has, "What *use* is it?" The understood answer is "*None.*" Faith without works is *useless.*

James does not deny that this man has faith. The trouble was that the man's faith was expressed only in *talking.* He knew the *vocabulary* of faith, but not the *vocation* of faith. He could *talk* it but he didn't *walk* it. He was long on *profession* but short on *practice.* This type of faith, says James, is *useless.*

James now gives an illustration of talking but not doing: "If a brother or sister be naked, and destitute of daily food, and one of you say unto them, Depart in peace, be ye warmed and filled; notwithstanding ye give them not those things which are needful to the body; what doth it profit? Even so faith, if it hath not works, is dead, being alone" (James 2:15-17).

Here is a brother or sister in Christ, one with whom you share the very closest of relationships. This one is "naked"—without adequate clothing. And "destitute of daily food"—desperately *hungry.* These are not professional bums. These are genuinely and desperately in need. They lack those things "*needful* to the body"—the most elementary needs, not luxuries but the very necessities of life. And their need *shows.* I can see them standing there in their rags with the cold winds whistling about them and the snowflakes beginning to swirl about their emaciated bodies. Their faces are gaunt and drawn and their skin has the dry scaly look of dehydration. Without help, they cannot last long upon this earth. And what is the response? "Depart in peace, be ye warmed and filled!"

"Depart in peace" was the standard Jewish farewell. It was roughly equivalent to our cheery, "Have a good day!" "Be ye warmed and filled" just meant "I surely hope your needs are taken care of." *But the man did nothing to take care of those needs.* He didn't share what he had; he didn't pull out his wallet; he didn't say, "You can use my credit card"; he didn't even get them in touch with the deacon in charge of benevolence. He just sent them off with *words*—cold, empty, useless, meaningless words. What did this profit? *Nothing.* You can't wrap words around a shivering body. There are no calories in words. Words without works are worthless, useless!

So James concludes this point: "Even so faith, if it hath not works, is *dead being alone*" (verse 17). This kind of faith is a lifeless corpse—dead and useless!

## II. FAITH WITHOUT WORKS CANNOT BE DEMONSTRATED.
### Verse 18.

With James hitting so close to home, one might expect objections. He anticipates one in verse 18: "Yea, a man may say, Thou hast faith, and I have works: show me thy faith without thy works, and I will show thee my faith by my works." James' answer is clear: There is no way for a man to demonstrate his faith except by *doing* something.

We understand this in other areas of life. What if a desperate criminal were to point a gun at me and say, "Put up your hands or I'll shoot"? How would I show that I believed him? By putting up my hands! What if the doctor said, "Take this medicine and you'll get well"? How could I show that I believe him? By taking the medicine! And this is just as true in the spiritual realm as it is in life in general!

## III. FAITH WITHOUT WORKS CANNOT CHANGE A PERSON.
### Verses 19, 20.

The Jewish background of many of his readers seems to be in James' mind as he starts his next point: "Thou believest that there is one God; thou doest well. . . ." (James 2:19a). The Jews prided themselves on their belief in *one* God. The Shema, the classic statement that "The Lord our God is one Lord" (Deuteronomy 6:4), was echoed by every faithful Jew morning and evening and continually in the temple.

James does not hesitate to commend them on their belief in one God: "Thou doest well." But he then quickly lets his readers know that faith did not make them unique: "The *devils* [or demons] also believe and tremble" (James 2:19b; emphasis mine). Demons are the devil's underlings and coworkers. Demons believe in the one God (James 2:19). They believe in the deity of Jesus (Mark 3:11, 12). They believe in the existence of a place of punishment (Luke 8:30, 31). They believe in Christ as Judge (Mark 5:1-13).

Believing all this, they *tremble*. The root of the Greek word translated "tremble" is "to bristle" or to have one's hair stand on end (see Job 4:14). These demons know what is ahead and it *terrifies* them!

But that's as far as it goes with demons. There's much I don't know about demons, but *this* I know: Even after they believe and tremble *they remain demons*, still Satan's henchmen, not angels serving God! Faith without works will not, cannot, change a person! So again, James hammers home his point: "But wilt thou know, O vain man [literally, empty-headed man] that faith without works is dead" (James 2:20).

# IV. FAITH WITHOUT WORKS IS
# NOT PERFECTED.
## Verses 21-25.

There would be no individual more respected by James' Jewish Christian readers than "Father Abraham." James calls upon the life of Abraham for proof of his thesis that faith must work in order to please God: "Was not Abraham our father justified by works, when he had offered Isaac his son upon the altar? Seest thou how faith wrought with his works, and by works was faith made perfect? And the scripture was fulfilled which saith, Abraham believed God, and it was imputed unto him for righteousness: and he was called the Friend of God. Ye see then how that by works a man is justified, and not by faith only" (James 2:21-24).

Every little Jewish boy and girl knew by heart the story of Abraham offering Isaac (Genesis 22:11-19). To test Abraham, God came to him and told him to take his son, his only son of promise, Isaac, into the land of Moriah and there to offer him as a burnt offering. Early the next day Abraham, Isaac, and two young male servants started on the journey. On the third day they reached the designated spot, a mountain. The two servants were left behind while Abraham and Isaac climbed the mountain. They took with them the wood, the fire, and the knife for the burnt offering. As they toiled upward, Isaac asked, "My father . . . Behold the fire and the wood: but where is the lamb for a burnt offering?" (Genesis 22:7). Abraham's heart must have been breaking, but he replied, "My son, God will provide" (Genesis 22:8).

At last they reached the summit. Abraham built the altar, put on the wood, and then bound Isaac and laid him on the altar. I cannot imagine the feelings of father and son as this was done nor what words might have passed between them. Abraham then took the knife to slay his son. There was no hesitation. In his heart he had already done the deed

(Hebrews 11:17). But a Voice from heaven stopped him, saying, "Now I *know* that thou fearest God, seeing thou hast not withheld thy son, thine only son from me" (Genesis 22:12; emphasis mine). Abraham was allowed to substitute a ram, caught in a nearby thicket, for his son—and then the Voice came again, repeating the great covenant promise first made in Genesis 18:1-3. It concluded: "And in thy seed shall all the nations of the earth be blessed; *because thou hast obeyed my voice*" (Genesis 22:18; emphasis mine).

How was Abraham able to meet such a test? Because he had *faith*, the kind of faith that *did what God said* even though he did not fully understand.

This is a nice straightforward illustration, establishing the point that the only viable faith is the faith that obeys. I'm sure James would be astonished if he could hear the objections his illustration prompts.

The word "justifies" disturbs many. One says, "This means that he was justified *in the eyes of men* when he offered Isaac." But no one else was present on the occasion mentioned except Abraham and Isaac and God. Another says, the justification referred to here is not the initial justification of one becoming a child of God, but rather *ultimate* justification. But Paul quotes the same passage that James does (Genesis 15:6) and applies it to initial justification (Romans 4:1-4).

But someone says, "Works *can't* have anything to do with going to heaven! In Romans 4 Paul gives a different illustration of Abraham's faith and says in effect that Abraham was *not* justified by works (verse 2)!" But, as already noted, Paul and James do not contradict each other. Rather their statements are complementary, supplementary. In context, Paul is talking about works of merit, such as those under the Law of Moses, whereby a person is trying to *earn* his salvation by a good life, by helping others, or other good deeds. On the other hand, James is talking about works that emulate from a heart that simply wants to *do* what God says, with no thought of earning or meriting anything.

Exactly what *does* James say? Let's look briefly at the text:

Verse 21—Abraham was *justified* by works, when he offered Isaac. He was justified (or counted as righteous— verse 23) by God *when* he obeyed.

Verse 22a—"Faith *wrought with* his works." "Wrought with" is literally "worked with" or *cooperated.* Faith and works *cooperated.* James doesn't teach "faith only." James doesn't teach "works only." James teaches faith *and* works.

Verse 22b—"By works was faith made perfect"—or completed or finished. Our faith *needs* to be perfected— and this is the purpose of works.

Verse 23a—"The scripture was fulfilled which saith, Abraham believed God, and it was imputed unto him for righteousness." The word translated "imputed" is trans- lated "reckoned" or "counted" in other translations. It means *to credit to someone's account that which does not actu- ally belong to him.* Abraham was not righteous, just, perfect in every respect. But God *counted* Abraham as righteous, put it on the ledger that he was righteous, when Abraham believed.

And when did all this take place? The scripture referred to in verse 23 is Genesis 15:6. At the time referred to in that passage, Abraham had no children and he was growing old. But God told him that his children would be as numberless as the stars. We then read in Genesis 15:6: "And he *believed* in the Lord; and he [God] counted it to him for righteous- ness." (Emphasis mine.) But this event took place several years before Abraham offered Isaac. How do they tie together? James is saying that *the point at which* Abraham's faith was "counted for righteousness" was after that faith had been tested and met the test. It was *after* Abraham's obedience that God said, "Now I *know* that thou fearest God" (Genesis 22:12; emphasis mine; see also 22:18).

Verse 23b—"And he was called the Friend of God." This appellation was called on Abraham long after his death (Isaiah 41:8; II Chronicles 20:7). Why was Abraham "God's friend"? *Because he did what God said!!!*

Man may find these verses controversial, but it is obvious that James thinks this is a clear illustration. There can be only one conclusion: "*Ye see then how that by works a man is justified, and not by faith only*" (James 2:24).

But James is not finished. Some might say that Abraham was a child of God before he offered Isaac, so James' statement has nothing to do with becoming a child of God. Listen to James' last illustration: "Likewise also was not *Rahab the harlot* justified by works, when she had received the messengers and had sent them out another way?" (James 2:25; emphasis mine). The verse begins, "Likewise also." The NIV has "In the same way." James is talking about the same kind of faith, the same kind of justification.

One would be hard pressed to think of a greater contrast than that of Abraham and Rahab. One the father of the Jews, the other a Gentile. One godly, the other sinful. One the friend of God, the other among the enemies of God. But they had one thing in common. When they *believed*, their faith caused them to *act*.

Like the story of Abraham, the story of Rahab was a familiar one to the Jews. She is listed among the heroes of faith in Hebrews 11 (verse 31). She was the great-grandmother of David the King and in the lineage of Jesus Christ (Matthew 1:5, 6).

Her story is found in Joshua, chapters 2 and 6. When Joshua sent two spies into Jericho to determine its strength, they found a most unexpected ally in Rahab, the harlot. She had heard how God had been with the Israelites and she believed (Joshua 2:10, 11). At the risk of her own life, she bravely helped the spies to escape, using the well-known scarlet cord. As a result, when Jericho was destroyed, she and her family were spared as they followed the exact instructions of those spies.

By no stretch of the imagination could Rahab be spoken of as a child of God before she was "justified by works." The Hebrew word for "harlot" in the book of Joshua might be ambiguous but the Greek word in the books of James and Hebrews is not. She was a prostitute, a pagan living by pagan standards. But she came to *believe* in the one true and living God, and that faith caused her to *cooperate* in the plan of God. Her faith *did* something—and as a result she was spared, she was admitted to covenant relationship, her entire life was changed!

Let me pause now to ask you a question: Is there any comfort in this section on Abraham and Rahab for those who would say, "Just believe on the Lord, just say a little prayer and be saved"? I think I can hear your answer: None at all. But now let me ask you another question: Is there any comfort in this passage for the one who has been baptized, *whose faith has ceased to work?* It is very tempting when studying this passage to center our attack on those who teach error. But let us never forget that James' guns are zeroed in on his *brethren.* The point of this passage is, let us examine *ourselves*—*our* hearts, *our* obedience.

## V. IN SHORT, FAITH WITHOUT WORKS IS *DEAD.*
## Verse 26.

If we were to try to determine James' main point by the number of times it is repeated, it would be a toss-up between the fact that we are "justified by works" (verses 21, 24, 25) or that "faith without works is dead" (verses 17, 20, 26). James has just restated the former in verse 25. He now restates the latter: "For as the body without the spirit is dead, so faith without works is dead also" (verse 26).

Doctors and lawyers struggle with the question, at what point does *death* occur? When the heart stops beating? When the brain waves cease? When all bodily functions cease? Or when? James' answer may have little meaning in a court of law or a medical textbook, but it is decisive: Death occurs when the immortal spirit, given to us by the Father of Spirits (Hebrews 12:9; Ecclesiastes 12:7), leaves this mortal body, a gift from our parents.

Probably the best short and most concise definition of "death" as used in the Bible is the word "*separation.*" The body separated from the spirit is *dead.*

Even so, says James, in the matter of faith. "Faith without works is dead also." Faith separated from works is lifeless!

## FOR DISCUSSION

1. Some claim that James downgrades *faith* in this letter. Is this true (James 1:3; 2:1; 5:15)?
2. Discuss some ways that we can express our love for the brethren.
3. What does the Bible have to say about demons? (Were they real—or just physical or mental disorders, etc.?)
4. Contrast the *dead* faith of verses 17, 20, 26, the *demon's* faith of verse 19, and the *dynamic* faith that James says we *should* have.
5. Did Abraham actually sacrifice Isaac? If not, why does verse 21 say he did? See also Hebrews 11:17-19.
6. Do James' statements in verses 21 through 24 contradict Paul's statements in Romans 4:1-5?
7. Creed books say that we are "justified by faith only." What does James say?
8. Should we, however, confine our application of James 2:14-26 to those in *denominations* who teach error?
9. If we truly have *faith*, what will we do? To become Christians? As Christians?

# DANGER!
# TONGUE AT WORK!

*James 3:1-12*

There is no way to over-emphasize the importance of using the tongue properly. When we go to the doctor, it is not uncommon for him to say, "Stick out your tongue." He can tell much about our physical condition by looking at the tongue. Even so, it is possible to tell much about our *spiritual* health by looking at our tongues, or at least our use of them.

Christians in James' day were misusing the vast power of tongue and James did not hesitate to tell them so. Some feel that James uses much exaggeration and hyperbole in this section, but the longer I live and deal with people, the less I am inclined to believe that James exaggerates at all. The tongue is a powerful force—and, misused, can destroy lives!

We need to do all we can to keep our tongues under control for five reasons:

## I. BECAUSE OF THE GREAT RESPONSIBILITY WE HAVE AS TEACHERS.
### Verses 1, 2.

James begins: "My brethren, be not many masters, knowing that we shall receive the greater condemnation.

For in many things we offend all. If any man offend not in word, the same is a perfect man, and able also to bridle the whole body" (James 3:1, 2).

The word "masters" refers to "*school*masters." The Greek word here is the word for "teachers." James' opening statement is therefore startling: "My brethren, be not many [teachers]!" At first glance, this appears to contradict other passages in the New Testament (Matthew 28:18-20; Hebrews 5:12). Why would James command that many of them should not be teachers?

Let me suggest, first of all, that James is talking about a distinctive ministry, that spoken of when Paul said, "And he gave . . . some, evangelists; and some, pastors [or elders] *and teachers*" (Ephesians 4:11; emphasis mine). This ministry refers to the "public" teaching of the word, such as is done in our Bible classes. Every Christian should be involved in sharing Christ and His word with others (Acts 8:1, 4), but not every Christian is required to be a teacher on a more formal basis.

But this raises another question: Is James saying that most of us should not aspire to be public teachers?? We always seem to be in need of good, qualified teachers! No, neither is James trying to discourage those who would desire to teach classes. Rather James is emphasizing two things:

(1) *Do not become teachers from the wrong motivation.*

Among the Jewish people, it was a great honor to be a rabbi or teacher. In the New Testament church, the public teacher of the word also held an exalted position—along with the apostles, prophets, evangelists, and elders (Ephesians 4:11). People being people, there would be some who would desire the *position* of teacher for the *honor* it might bring. Some find it hard to resist the combination of position, prominence, and plaudits!

(2) *Do not become teachers without preparing yourselves.*

Verse 13 of the chapter has: "Who is a wise man and endued with knowledge among you? let him *show* out of a good conversation [manner of life] his works with meekness of wisdom." (Emphasis mine.) Obviously some were *claiming* to be wise and endued with knowledge. James challenges them to *prove* their claims. They evidently wanted to be acclaimed as wise and knowledgeable teachers without going to the trouble of preparing themselves.

The influence of a teacher is so great that it is imperative that each teacher prepare himself or herself in mind and life. This involves gaining a knowledge of God's word (I Timothy 1:7). This involves training in *how* to teach. And it involves *living* by the standards that we proclaim (Romans 2:17-19; II Timothy 2:2).

Why does James warn against becoming teachers for the wrong reasons and without adequate preparation? Verse 1 concludes: "Knowing that we shall receive the greater condemnation." Or as the ASV puts it, "Knowing that we shall receive *heavier judgment.*"

The teacher of God's word has great blessings in this life (Philippians 4:1; III John 4) and in the next (Daniel 12:3), but he also has great responsibilities. If he fails in his task, both he and those he teaches can be lost!

But for what will we be judged as teachers? Verse 2 begins, "For in many things we offend all"—or, we all offend. "Offend" refers to offending God by breaking His laws. We all fall short of being what we should be. Do any need proof of this? James goes at once to an area in which all of us are deficient: "If any man offend not in *word*, the same is a perfect man, and able also to bridle the whole body" (verse 2b; emphasis mine).

"Perfect" means "complete" or "mature." This is the goal of every Christian. Christian maturity is directly tied to the ability to control the tongue. The one who can control his tongue can control his thoughts (Matthew 12:34b) and the one who can control his actions, thus can "bridle the whole body."

So we have come to the subject of the *tongue.*

# II. BECAUSE OF THE POWER OF THE TONGUE.
## Verses 3-5a.

This section of James is filled with visual images. Three comparisons are made in the next three verses to impress a single lesson: *The power of little things*:

"Behold we put bits in the horses' mouths, that they may obey us; and we turn about their whole body. Behold also the ships, which though they are great, and are driven of fierce winds, yet are they turned about with a very small helm, whithersoever the governor listeth. Even so the tongue is a small member, and boasteth great things. Behold, how great a matter a little fire kindleth!" (James 3:3-5).

James' first illustration refers to putting a bit in the horse's mouth to be able to turn about the horse's body. The average horse is large—about one-half ton of muscle, bones, and sinews. On the other hand, a bit is small—a few ounces of steel fashioned where it will fit into the horse's mouth. But because the horse's mouth is tender, those few ounces of steel can be used to direct the horse in one direction or another.

The second illustration is that of the power of a small rudder over a large ship. "The helm" refers to the rudder, a steering paddle or oar sticking out the back of the ship. The "governor" was the steersman, the man sitting in the back of the ship moving the rudder from one side to the other. Regardless of the size of the ship, the helmsman could move the small rudder just a little and the whole ship would change its direction.

"Even so," says James, "the tongue is a little member" (verse 5). It is not as big as a leg, a foot, an arm, or a hand. It is only a few ounces of muscle in a body weighing many pounds. But this does not mean that it is weak. Like the little bit and the little rudder, the little tongue is *powerful*. James says, it "boasteth great things" (verse 5). This is not referring to idle boasts, but what the tongue actually can accomplish.

The tongue has the potential of great good or great evil. The wise man said, "*Death* and *life* are in the power of the tongue" (Proverbs 18:21; emphasis mine). On the negative side, we might think of the words of Hitler that inflamed a nation. For every word in Hitler's book, *Mein Kampf*, 125 lives were lost in World War II. On the positive side, we might think of the words of Churchill that strengthened a nation, and inspired the world!

## III. BECAUSE OF THE POTENTIAL OF THE TONGUE FOR *EVIL.*
### Verses 5b, 6.

James now gives a third illustration of the power of small things, this time an illustration of the power of little things to *destroy*: "Behold, how great a matter a little fire kindleth! And the tongue is a fire, a world of iniquity: so is the tongue among our members, that it defileth the whole body, and setteth on fire the course of nature; and it is set on fire of hell" (James 3:5b, 6).

The ASV begins this section, "How much wood is kindled by how small a fire." Our minds go back to the Great Fire in Chicago in 1871 where the fire raged for 24 hours, hours of horror. The damage has been estimated at $400 million. The same day the Chicago fire broke out, a forest fire started in Wisconsin, killing 1,152 persons!

Fire, when controlled, can warm us, cook our food, and cheer us as it crackles in the fireplace. Even so the tongue under control can bless, cheer, and gladen the heart. But on the other hand, a fire out of control in a matter of minutes can destroy that which took months or years to build and grow. So it is with the tongue. Out of control, it can blight, destroy, and damn. Then it becomes the hellish thing spoken of in verse 6:

"And the tongue is a fire, a world of iniquity: so is the tongue among our members, and it defileth the whole body, and setteth on fire the course of nature; and it is set on fire of hell."

James uses the most flamboyant phrases in this verse to get across the devastating nature of the tongue unchecked. It is "a world of iniquity" (verse 6b). It encompasses *all kinds* of iniquity. Phillips' translation has this rendering: "with *vast potentialities* for evil."

Every type of sin can be tied with the tongue: (1) Sins against God, such as blasphemy (Exodus 20:7). Or cursing (Romans 3:10, 13, 14). (2) Sins against *others*, such as lying (Proverbs 12:22). Or bearing false witness (Proverbs 19:5). Or gossiping and talebearing (Proverbs 16:27, 28). (3) Sins against *oneself*, such as "grievous words" that can get one in trouble (Proverbs 15:1). Or "corrupt words" that reveal one's heart (Ephesians 4:29). Or just too much talk (Proverbs 10:19).

This thought of sins of the tongue affecting the *owner* of that tongue seems to be uppermost in James' mind as he continues in the text: "So is the tongue among our members, that it defileth the whole body" (verse 6c).

A fire not only destroys and consumes all within its immediate reach; it also stains, pollutes, and defiles everything around it for some distance. So it is with the tongue. The tongue is not isolated from the other members of the body. What the tongue does, affects the whole man. No man is better than his word. So the NEB says that the wrong use of the tongue "pollutes our whole being."

And we are not talking about a one-time thing, an occasional occurrence. The untamed tongue affects *all* of life. James' cryptic way of saying this is: "And [it] setteth on fire the course of nature" (verse 6d). The Greek text has "the *wheel* of nature." Most of James' readers would have been aware that in the Old Testament, *life* was compared with a wheel (Ecclesiastes 12:6). James' point is that all the time the "wheel" is turning, *i.e., throughout life*, the untamed tongue can blight and destroy like a fire out of control.

And what is the source of the devastation fanned by the tongue? James pulls no punches. "It is set on fire of *hell*" (verse 6e). The word translated "hell" is *gehenna*, the word for hell fire, the eternal abode of the wicked. When the Holy Spirit wanted to convey how terrible an uncontrolled tongue is, the only adequate word was the awful place of fire and brimstone, the place of eternal darkness, the ultimate abode of Satan and all who follow him (Matthew 25)!!

## IV. BECAUSE OF THE "UNTAMEABLE" NATURE OF THE TONGUE.
## Verses 7, 8.

"For every kind of beasts, and of birds, and of serpents, and of things in the sea, is tamed, and hath been tamed of mankind: But the tongue can no man tame; it is an unruly evil, full of deadly poison" (James 3:7, 8).

Having seen how devastating the tongue can be, this statement is alarming: "But the tongue can no man tame"!

All other creatures have been tamed. James gives four classifications encompassing all types of animated life: "Every kind of *beasts*" has been tamed. My mind goes to the Ringling Brothers, Barnum and Bailey Circus, and the amazing things that the dogs, bears, horses, elephants, and tigers do. And "every kind . . . of *birds*" has been tamed. Now I think of a live demonstration of trained birds that can roller-skate, fly on command, and do other remarkable things.

And "every kind . . . of *serpents*" has been tamed. The snake is a natural enemy of mankind (Genesis 3:14, 15cf.); what an unlikely creature to be tamed! But the snake-charmer of the East does exercise control over his serpent, guiding the snake as he rises slowly from the basket. And "every kind . . . of things in the *sea*." The memory now evokes scenes where dolphins, small whales, seals, and sea lions have been trained to perform almost every trick imaginable through the proper use of love, discipline, rewards, and patience. But, in contrast to these, James says, "The *tongue* can no man tame."

To illustrate how deadly it is, James compares the tongue to a *snake*: "It is an unruly evil, full of deadly poison" (verse 8b). This is the last comparison with a little thing in our text. Most venomous snakes are small but the poison deposited in the pockets under their mouths can kill!

Think of a snake silently slithering through the undergrowth until it *strikes*, driving its venom deep within its victim, and then crawling swiftly away. Thus do some use their tongues! There are some who would never think of turning loose a sack full of snakes in the church auditorium, who think nothing of whispering their innuendoes and slander, destroying reputations within those same four walls!

Should we therefore give up? After all James has said, "The tongue can no man tame." No, God expects us to control our tongues. Remember James 1:26: "If any man among you seem to be religious, and bridleth not his tongue, but deceiveth his own heart, this man's religion is vain." In 3:10 James says, "My brethren, these things *ought not so to be.*" (Emphasis mine.) He would not have made such a statement if we could not help whether the things were so or not.

What then is James' point when he says, "The tongue can no man tame"? The key is found in several words in the statement. Perhaps there is significance in the word "tame": We may not be able to *tame* the tongue, but we can learn to *control* it.

These suggestions have been given on how we can control our tongues: (1) We can work on our *hearts* for "out of the abundance of the *heart* the mouth speaketh" (Matthew 12:34; emphasis mine). (2) We can learn to use *wisdom* in our use of the tongue—as did the worthy woman of Proverbs 31 (verse 26). (3) If all else fails, we can *keep our mouths shut*: "And . . . study [give diligence] *to be quiet*" (I Thessalonians 4:11; emphasis mine; see also I Peter 3:10; Ecclesiastes 3:7).

But probably the most significant word in the sentence is the word "man": "The tongue can no *man* tame." Remember Matthew 19:26: "But Jesus . . . said unto them, With *men* this is impossible; but with God all things are possible." (Emphasis mine.) There is help from *above*.

Think of John, one of the "sons of thunder," who became the Apostle of Love. He didn't do that on his own. He had help from God. Or Peter who cursed and swore when denying Jesus. But with the help of the Lord, he grew and matured spiritually; thus we never read of him misusing his tongue in that way again! In our struggle to control our tongues, we must stay as close to the Lord as we can. As David prayed: "Set a watch, O Lord, before my mouth; keep the door of my lips" (Psalm 141:3).


# V. BECAUSE OF THE INCONSISTENCIES OF THE TONGUE.
## Verses 9-12.

"Therewith bless we God, even the Father; and therewith curse we man, which are made after the similitude of God. Out of the same mouth proceedeth blessing and cursing. My brethren, these things ought not so to be. Doth a fountain send forth at the same place sweet water and bitter? Can the fig tree, my brethren, bear olive berries? either a vine, figs? so can no fountain both yield salt water and fresh" (James 3:9-12).

The word "bless" is used in the sense of prayer, praise, and adoration. The NIV has, "With the tongue we praise our Lord and Father." The English word "curse" originally meant "to invoke evil by the sign of the cross." These were praising God and at the same wishing evil upon men—men made in God's likeness!

Perhaps we immediately think of some who give lip service to Jesus, but whose mouths at the same time are a constant flowing sewer. How repulsive! But let us not fail to ask: Can *we* as the people of God ever be guilty of this same type of inconsistency? To be very personal: Picture the family singing praises together in the assembly—and then fussing and fighting in the car all the way home! James thunders, "My brethren, these things ought not so to be" (verse 10b)!

James has stressed that "these things ought not so to be" because such things are *unscriptural*. Now he makes the point that "these things ought not so to be" because such is *unnatural*: "Doth a fountain send forth at the same place sweet water and bitter? Can the fig tree, my brethren, bear olive berries? either a vine, figs? so can no fountain both yield salt water and fresh" (James 3:11, 12).

Palestine abounded with fountains, wells, and springs. Most were filled with pure, sweet water. But some, especially those near the Dead Sea, were filled with brackish water—as the salty water seeped through the soil. But *none* gave forth both fresh, sweet water and salty, bitter water at the same time. Nature is consistent.

Palestine also abounded in fig trees and grapevines; most yards had one or both. So his readers would readily comprehend James' meaning as he asked: "Can the fig tree . . . bear olive berries? either a vine, figs?"

Nature is consistent. Unfortunately man is not always so. There are no two-watered fountains. There are no natural two-fruited trees. But there *are* two-faced men. May God help us not to be spiritual Dr. Jekylls and Mr. Hydes. "These things ought not so to be"!

## FOR DISCUSSION

1. Should any desire to become a teacher because of the pres-

tige it might offer? Note Matthew 23:8, 11.

2. Should one be allowed to teach a class who does not attend all the services of the church and who does not show an interest in all the activities of the church?

3. Since James says that teachers will receive the heavier judgment, can one escape that judgment by *not* teaching—*if* one has the potential to be a teacher?

4. Give examples of the *power* of the tongue in general.

5. Give examples of the potential of the tongue for *good*.

6. Give examples of the potential of the tongue for *evil*.

7. What is the difference between "taming" and "controlling"? What suggestions might you give on how to *control* the tongue?

8. Discuss the sin of cursing. Is it possible to separate our treatment of God and our treatment of our fellow man (I John 4:20)?

9. Can chronic blasphemers control their speech under certain conditions (around their mothers, preachers, or whatever)? Could they then control their speech all the time?

10. What do you consider the greatest need in the matter of using our tongues as we should?

# YOU, TOO, CAN BE WISE!

*James 3:13-18*

It doesn't matter how high or how low your I.Q. is. It doesn't matter how experienced or inexperienced you may be. It doesn't matter how much or how little formal education you have. You can be wise *with the wisdom that counts*. Follow James' thought carefully to discover what *true* wisdom is, and thus how you can be wise:

## I. TRUE WISDOM FINDS EXPRESSION.
### Verse 13.

James begins: "Who is a wise man and endued with knowledge among you? Let him show out of a good conversation his works with meekness of wisdom" (verse 13).

James is primarily directing his attention to public teachers of the word. The chapter begins with these words: "My brethren, be not many masters [literally, *teachers*]" (verse 1). Now James asks: "Who is a wise man and endued with knowledge among you?" The term "wise" man was often used in the scriptures to refer to one who was a teacher (see Luke 10:21cf.; I Corinthians 1:20; etc.). "Endued with knowledge" was also used to describe the sharer of information. Robertson says that in this context the first word "is used for the practical teacher" and the second "for an expert, a skilled and scientific person with a tone of superiority." So James is asking, "Who among you makes the claim of being a wise and skillful teacher, an expert in this field?"

Let me stress that these qualities are good and most needed. We *need* wise and skilled teachers (Proverbs 4:7), even experts. But the context shows that these wanted to be *considered* as wise, skillful, expert teachers without really being such. "Who is a wise man and endued with knowledge among you? *Let him show out of a good conversation* [literally, a good life] *his works* with meekness of wisdom."

The world has many tests for wisdom. There is the I.Q. test—that measures intelligence. There is the paper test—how many degrees you may or may not have. There is the verbal test—whether you can demonstrate a shrewd mind by your sharp tongue and ready wit. But James says that the test that matters is the *life* test: Can you show *by your good life* that you are truly wise?

James immediately mentions one practical way to tell if our wisdom is genuine or not: "Let him show out of a good conversation [life] his works *with meekness of wisdom.*" The ones James is addressing were apparently arrogant with their claims to superiority. James says that those who are truly wise are *meek.*

Meekness is not weakness. "Meek" is the word the Greeks used to refer to a horse that had been broken to ride. It signified harnessed and directed strength. One writer calls it "gentle strength." The truly wise person has nothing to prove to the world. He can be meek, humble, unassuming.

How does one *show* that he is wise? To make clear what true wisdom really is, James spends the remainder of the passage contrasting true wisdom and wisdom-so-called.

## II. THE WISDOM OF THIS WORLD.
### Verses 14-16.

James begins with the negative: "But if ye have bitter envying and strife in your hearts, glory not, and lie not against the truth. This wisdom descendeth not from above, but is earthly, sensual, devilish. For where envying and strife is, there is confusion and every evil work" (James 3:14-16). Three points of contrast are given:

A. ORIGIN. "This wisdom," says James, "descendeth not from above, but is earthly, sensual, devilish" (verse 15). This is the wisdom-so-called, that which poses as wisdom but is not. This "wisdom" is *not* from above, not from God, but is rather: "Earthly"—it is of this earth, not of heaven. "Sensual"—it appeals to the flesh, to the "natural" man. "Devilish" (literally "demonic")—its ties are with Satan and his cohorts!

This is not true wisdom but poses as wisdom *by using the designation of wisdom*. The Greek word for wisdom is *sophos*—which has become a part of our vocabulary in some very common words:

There, for instance, is the word *"philosophy."* This is a combination of two Greek words—*philou* ("love of") and *sophus* ("wise"). It indicates "a love of wisdom." Philosophy is not wrong or bad within itself, but too much of what is called "philosophy" today is a perversion of God's truth about man and the universe in which he lives. No matter how learned an individual may be, if he leaves God and His word out of his reasoning, his conclusions must always be warped and deceptive!

Then there is the word *"sophisticated,"* directly derived from *sophos* or "wise." The dictionary gives the primary meaning of the word as "worldly-wise; deprived of natural simplicity; disillusioned." The secondary meaning is "pretentiously wise; possessing superficial information." Are not these phrases synonyms for the wisdom that is earthly and sensual? Most of us could profitably learn a few more of the social graces, but let us never forget the warning of Paul in II Corinthians 11:3: "But I fear, lest . . . your minds should be corrupted from the *simplicity* that is in Christ." (Emphasis mine.)

But the word that probably comes closest to what James is talking about is the word "*sophistry.*" This word took on a certain meaning through the years because of the Greek Sophists who paraded as wise men, but who used logic and reasoning to their own ends. Thus the dictionary defines "sophistry" as "subtly fallacious [or deceptive] reasoning or disputation" and a "sophism" as "a false argument intentionally used to deceive."

Satan still has his subtle lies, posing as wisdom, and people still believe them because they want to: "It's OK to do it. Everybody else is." "If it feels good, do it. It can't be wrong if it feels so right." "You should be allowed to do anything you want to. After all, it's *your* life and you're not hurting anyone else."

This is wisdom that is "earthly, sensual, devilish," wisdom-so-called.

B. CHARACTERISTICS. The characteristics of this "wisdom" are found in verse 14: "But if ye have bitter envying and strife in your hearts, glory not, and lie not against the truth":

(1) *Jealous.* The first characteristic is "bitter envying" or "bitter jealousy" (ASV). Why should this be listed first? *Because worldly wisdom promotes self-interest.* Man has dethroned God in his life and enthroned himself. Therefore if someone has something *I* want, it is only natural that I should be filled with a consuming jealousy that produces a bitterness in my mouth, my stomach, my soul.

None of us is immune from the poison of jealousy, whether we be the little boy that asks his parents to take his baby brother "back where he came from," or whether we be the aging executive passed over for promotion.

(2) *Self-centered.* The next characteristic stresses that the wisdom of this world is self-centered. The Greek word

referred to the condition of heart of one who would stop at nothing to get what he wanted—one who would not hesitate to stir up trouble if he thought it would help his cause. The KJV translates the word as "strife", the RSV and others as "*selfish ambition.*"

In the first two characteristics, we have a combination of "selfish ambition" and "party spirit"—the attitude that says, "Promote yourself by any means and try to line up everybody on your side"! Is it possible that we have, at one time or another, succumbed to Satan's "wisdom" and have caused strife and trouble by trying to line up people as "for us" and "against us"?! Is it even possible that churches have been divided by men whose feelings have been hurt and who want to know, "Who will stand behind me?"!

(3) *Boastful.* The last part of verse 14 commands: "*Glory not.*" The RSV has "do not *boast.*" Guy N. Woods says that this means "to boast of one's affairs *to the hurt of another.*" If one is guided by worldly wisdom, he will be self-centered, envious of the success of others, and selfishly ambitious to promote his own cause. What more natural way to do this than by boasting? And how natural, while we are boasting, to run down others to make ourselves look even better!

(4) *Deceitful.* Finally James says, "*Lie not* against the truth." When the self-seeking, ambitious man begins to boast, first facts are exaggerated, then half-truths and selective truths appear, and finally he gets down to what Grandma called "bald-faced *lies.*"

C. RESULTS. "For where envying and strife is, there is confusion and every evil work" (verse 16). In what does this earthly wisdom result? The text gives two fruits:

(1) *Confusion.* The word translated "confusion" refers to the "disorder that comes from instability." It comes from the same root as the word "unstable" in James 1:8 and the word "unruly" in James 3:8.

(2) *Cheapness.* The KJV then refers to "every evil work." Some who are self-seeking will literally stop at nothing to accomplish their evil! But the word "evil" here is not

confined to that which is obviously ungodly. The ASV and RSV use the word "vile" instead of evil. The Greek word refers to that which is cheap, gaudy, worthless. This includes immorality, but also refers to the cheap, valueless things with which the worldly-wise must fill their lives.

## III. THE WISDOM FROM ABOVE.
## Verses 17, 18.

But now let us go to the positive. Let us see the wisdom that you can have, that every child of God can have, the true wisdom: "But the wisdom that is from above is first pure, then peaceable, gentle, and easy to be entreated, full of mercy and good fruits, without partiality, and without hypocrisy. And the fruit of righteousness is sown in peace of them that make peace" (James 3:17, 18). Again we note three points of contrast:

A. ORIGIN. The wisdom of this world is "earthly, sensual, devilish" (verse 15), but true wisdom "is from above" (verse 17). Without a closeness to God, any claim to wisdom is mistaken, untrue, and deceptive.

B. CHARACTERISTICS. The wisdom of this world is: (1) Jealous, (2) self-centered, (3) boastful, (4) deceitful. In contrast our text gives seven characteristics of true wisdom:

(1) *Pure.* James begins, "The wisdom that is from above is first pure." The word "pure" literally means "unmixed"—it does not have some good and some bad. It refers to singleness of purpose, putting God and His ways first (Matthew 6:33; 22:37). This fidelity to God is manifest in purity of heart and mind, in purity of teaching, in purity of life.

This purity is to be *first*: "*First* pure, *then* peaceable." There are those who believe in "peace at any price," and that there is no higher purpose than living at peace with all men. But James says that *purity* must be first on the list. Some think of themselves as peacemakers when in reality

73

they have signed a non-aggression pact with the devil. Peace that is procured by sacrificing one's convictions or the plain teaching of God's word can never have the approval of God.

(2) *Peaceable.* Following closely is the quality of being peaceable. Stress is placed in this passage on peace: "The fruit of righteousness is sown in peace of them that make peace" (verse 18).

It is unfortunate that there are those who have exalted peace above purity. It is also unfortunate that some, who proclaim their desire for doctrinal and moral purity have not learned how to be peaceable. In days past the battle cry for "Purity!" has been used to justify everything from the Spanish Inquisition to splitting churches over matters of opinion. It is not sufficient to have the message of God if we have the manner of Satan.

(3) *Gentle.* What is this thing called "gentleness"? The Amplified Bible uses three words to translate it: Courteous, considerate, gentle. As the loving mother deals gently with the bruised child, as the compassionate nurse deals gently with the suffering patient, so we need to deal gently, so gently with those with whom we come in contact. So many are emotionally bruised, spiritually suffering, looking for that gentle touch of genuine concern.

(4) *Open.* The fourth quality of the wisdom from above is described in these words: "Easy to be intreated." The RSV has, "open to reason." The one who has true wisdom does not think that there is nothing left for him to learn. The good teacher remains teachable; he has an open mind and an open heart.

The most important application of this quality is in our relationship with God: We must remain *open* to His will. But this quality is also important in our relationship with other people. This was in the minds of the KJV translators when they wrote, "*Easy* to be intreated." The truly wise person does not leave the impression that he knows it all. Rather he remains open to suggestions, instruction, even criticism (Proverbs 9:8).

(5) *Merciful.* The wisdom that is from above is "full of mercy and good fruits." "Mercy" refers to the capacity to be moved by the needs of others. But if it is true mercy, it will always result in "good fruits"—as we try to *help* those who are in need.

True "mercy" does not take into account the *worthiness* of the one in need. "Mercy" is closely related to "grace" or *unmerited* favor. It is easy to have mercy on one who is suffering through no fault of his own. It is not too hard to have mercy on one who is suffering because of his own mistakes, but who is truly sorry, truly penitent. But it is hard to have mercy on those who are suffering because of their own shortcomings, who are totally impenitent and who even blame others for their problems. And—it is hardest of all to have mercy on those who are suffering, who are blaming *us* for their troubles. But the truly wise remains "*full* of mercy and good fruits."

(6) *Consistent.* The KJV translates the sixth quality as "without partiality." But the quality spoken of here includes more than impartiality. The Amplified Bible uses no less than six words or phrases to try to express the complete thought: "Wholehearted and straightforward, impartial and unfeigned, free from doubts [and] wavering."

This is the opposite of the "confusion" that results from worldly wisdom (verse 16). This is the characteristic of a truly wise person who knows what he believes, knows why he believes it, and who lives in a manner consistent with those beliefs—completely dedicated to the Lord and completely fair in dealing with others. Some think they have convictions when really they just have closed minds. On the other hand there are those who think they have open minds when in reality they are merely gullible—lacking real stability, accepting almost anything (Ephesians 4:14).

It is not easy to have strong convictions and still remain open to reason, but the truly wise person has achieved that balance.

(7) *Sincere.* The final characteristic ties in with this consistency: The wisdom from above is "without hypocrisy." The word "hypocrisy" originally referred to wearing a mask as actors did in plays in those days. Some who wanted the position and prestige of being public teachers wore the masks of wisdom, understanding, and expertise. But those who were truly wise needed no such pretense. They had paid the price in preparation—preparation of heart, preparation of life, preparation of mind, preparation of skills. They were precisely what they appeared to be.

C. RESULT. The last contrast is the result: "And the fruit of righteousness is sown in peace of them that make peace" (verse 18). The fruit of earthly wisdom is "confusion and every evil work" (verse 16). The fruit of heavenly wisdom is "righteousness." In this context, righteousness refers to *a good life.* If one is truly wise, the result will be a beautiful, God-pleasing life.

James uses an illustration he has used before—that of sowing seed:

(1) The *sowers* are "them that make peace."

(2) The *proper growing condition* is peace: "Righteousness is sown *in peace.*" Proper growing conditions are necessary to the germination and growth of a seed. Righteousness cannot grow where there is confusion and every evil work. But in an atmosphere of peace with God and man, righteousness can thrive.

(3) The *seed* planted is righteousness itself. In plants that bear fruit, the seed is usually to be found in the fruit. In some cases (as in planting potatoes), in order to plant the seed, we actually plant the fruit. What is the point? Like begets like. One person living a righteous life will inspire others to live righteous lives.

(4) Thus the *fruit* produced is righteousness—a life that produces peace, uplifts men, and pleases God!

In closing let me return to the theme originally proposed: "You, too, can be wise." Develop whatever intellectual capacity God has given you; this is part of being good stewards of our blessings. But more importantly gain *the wisdom that really counts*. You can do this . . .

(1) By going to the right source. This wisdom is "from above." Stay close to God by Bible study, prayer, and meditation, and by close association with God's people.

(2) By developing the right qualities of life. Think of others more and yourself less. Strive to be pure, peaceable, gentle, open, merciful, consistent, and sincere.

(3) By aiming for the right result. Earthly popularity and success are fleeting and disillusioning. Make it your goal to be right in the sight of God and to live the God-pleasing life, a life of righteousness.

## FOR DISCUSSION

1. Discuss the difference between true wisdom and the wisdom of this world. Include I Corinthians 1:18-24 in your discussion.

2. Worldly wisdom is "devilish" (verse 15). Discuss how the devil has and does deceive mankind with his lies (Genesis 3:1-6; I John 2:16cf.).

3. Discuss the need for a balance between the qualities of "purity" and being "peaceable."

4. Discuss the need for *America* to have these qualities of "wisdom from above" (Proverbs 14:34) . . . The need in the church . . . The need in our individual lives (see the personal quiz on the next page).

5. Bible teachers need many qualities to be most efficient. According to James 3, however, what are the *most important* qualities?

6. This lesson clams that all of us can be "wise with the wisdom that counts." Can all of us develop the qualities mentioned— if we want to badly enough?

## AM I TRULY WISE?

(1) Do I put moral and doctrinal purity above all else?
( ) Yes;   ( ) No;   (🗸) I don't know.

(2) Am I easy to get along with—and do I try to promote peace and happiness wherever I am?
(🗸) Yes;   ( ) No;   ( ) I don't know.

(3) Do I try to be kind and considerate to others?
(🗸) Yes;   ( ) No;   ( ) I don't know.

(4) Am I "approachable"? Am I "teachable"? Do people feel free to come and talk to me (because I have not built a "shell" of defensiveness about myself)?
( ) Yes;   ( ) No;   ( ) I don't know.

(5) Do I have compassion for others—and do I *show* it by my actions?
( ) Yes;   ( ) No;   ( ) I don't know.

(6) Am I able to treat all men as *brothers*?
( ) Yes;   ( ) No;   ( ) I don't know.

(7) Am I *consistent* in my life?
( ) Yes;   ( ) No;   ( ) I don't know.

# WARS, WORLDLINESS, AND GOD'S WILL

*James 4:1-10*

It would be hard to imagine a more attention-getting opening than the question with which James begins chapter 4: "From whence come wars and fightings. . . ?" (verse 1).

"Where do wars come from? Why do we have to have wars?" The little boy looks at a scene of slaughter on the television set, then looks up at his father and asks, "Daddy, why do people fight?" The woman, burying her only son, tries to be brave, but as the tears stream down her cheeks, she is screaming inside, "Why? Why do we have to have wars?!"

Scholars have spent many years analyzing the underlying causes and the stated reasons for wars. They have discussed wars fought for land on which to live, wars fought to increase wealth and power, wars fought to protect one's borders. But what is the inspired answer? Read carefully James 4:1-4. James says that "wars and fightings" come *from within*—from the "lusts that war in your members." It may be lust for power, lust for pleasure, lust for prestige, lust for position, lust for possessions. When you get enough people together with all their lusts pointing in the direction of war, war is inevitable.

But James is not concerned about wars in general. He is concerned about "wars and fighting" much closer to home:

"From whence come wars and fightings *among you?*" His great concern is for fighting *among members of the body of Christ.*

Through the years there have been "wars" in the context of the church—often battles for the truth, but sometimes battles with less worthy motivations; such as the You-defeated-my-pet-project War, the They-won't-let-me-teach War, the They-fired-my-favorite-preacher War. Wars between nations are tragic, but nothing is more tragic than a religious "civil war" with brother arrayed against brother.

But again, James' emphasis is not on war, but on the lusts that produce "wars and fightings." James uses the subject of wars to get our attention, then concentrates on the subject of *worldliness.* His main thrust is on an attitude toward the world that results in problems in the church and in the life of the individual Christian. Taking my cue from James, it will be my purpose to discuss *the curse, the cause,* and *the cure* of worldliness.

## I. THE CURSE OF WORLDLINESS.
## Verses 1, 4.

Three different wars are discussed in this text: There is war with God (verse 4). There is war with others, especially those in the church (verse 1). Finally, there is the most crucial war of all—the war within the individual himself (verse 1). These three categories summarize how worldliness hurts:

First, worldliness hurts God and His cause. "Know ye not that the friendship of the world is enmity with God?" (verse 4). Nothing hurts the cause of God like those who are supposed to be His children living no differently from those in the world.

Second, worldliness hurts the church. Many people become dissatisfied with what the world has to offer, so they come to the church to see what the church has to offer—but far too often all they find is more of the world! Third, worldliness hurts the individual himself. Persisted in, it will damn his soul!

But what is this "worldliness" that hurts so much? The word "world" can refer to the physical world—the earth, the grass, the flowers, the birds. It can refer to the people in the world—"God so loved the world" (John 3:16). Or it can refer to the things in this world that appeal to the flesh as opposed to the spirit. "Worldliness" has reference to this last definition and means *exalting the things of this world above the things of God.* To most of us, a "worldly" person is one who engages in certain immoral acts, when in reality we might never engage in those particular acts, and still be a very worldly person.

How hard it is to keep from being overwhelmed by this world. We can get so involved in the things of this life that the things of God become of little importance. Someone once said that "Ford has made more atheists than Ingersoll, for Ingersoll just tried to appeal to men's minds while Ford gave them something else to occupy their time." Today, the same could be said for those who invented and perfected the television set—and other modern time-fillers and killers!

As we speak of "worldliness" in this lesson, let us be aware that we are talking about immorality, but let us also be aware that we are talking about a general attitude toward this world that can slowly but surely destroy our relationship with God. With this as a background, let us turn to our text to discover the *cause* and *cure* of worldliness.

## II. THE CAUSE OF WORLDLINESS.
## Verses 1-5.

The first four or five verses of our text give us the cause of worldliness. Read again verses 1 through 4, noticing the emphasis on *self*. Fourteen times in four verses, the second person "you" or "your" is used. All that is necessary to become a worldly person is to elevate SELF:

(1) *Want things for SELF.* Verses 1, 2a.

In the original language, each of the words translated "lust" or "desire" in verses 1 and 2 is a different word. The first word (verse 1) is the word for "pleasures," the word from which we get "hedonism," living for pleasure. The second word (verse 2) is the usual word for "desire." Here it refers to *unlawful* desires. The third word (verse 2) is the word for being "jealous" or "envious." I'm jealous of another; I want what he has. The picture is of a totally selfish person who is not concerned about others or God; he wants what *he* wants, to gratify his every wish.

(2) *Elevate SELF above God.* Verse 2.

And how does the worldly-minded person attempt to satisfy those desires? By any means at his disposal. Verse 2 says, "ye kill" and "ye fight and war." These words are used figuratively for the infighting that takes place when someone wants his own way and will cut down anyone who stands in the way. Such a person has left God out of his plans. Instead of trusting in self, he should have trusted in God. "Ye have not, because ye ask not." *Prayer* is more important than *power.*

(3) *Think only of SELF in your prayers.* Verse 3.

In verse 3, James anticipates an objection. He has just said, "Ye have not, because ye ask not." One can then imagine someone responding, "But I *did* ask. I asked God to give me that raise. I asked God to give me a bigger house . . . a lakeside cottage . . . a boat. So don't tell *me* I didn't ask!" James' response is that when you *do* ask, you ask with the wrong motives: "Ye ask, and receive not, because ye ask amiss, that ye may consume it upon your lusts" (verse 3).

The purpose of prayer is not so much to get our will done in heaven as it is to get God's will done on earth. Some think of God as an indulgent old grandfather whose only purpose is to satisfy their every whim! Their prayers are totally self-centered—not concerned with others, not concerned with the will and work of God—but concerned with what they desire.

(4) *Allow SELF to be deceived by the world.* Verse 4.

James gets to the heart of the problem in verse 4: "Ye adulterers and adulteresses, know ye not that the friendship of the world is enmity with God? Whosoever therefore will be a friend of the world is the enemy of God."

Adultery, an illicit sexual relationship, is severely condemned throughout the Bible (I Corinthians 6:10, 18). But physical adultery is not what James is primarily concerned about. The original text has only "adulteresses." Why? Because James is using the word "adulteresses" in a figurative sense. He is writing to members of *the church* and the church is pictured as the *bride* of Christ (II Corinthians 11:2; Romans 7:1ff.; Ephesians 6:31, 32cf.). James is saying that the church, Christ's bride, has been unfaithful to Christ, has been guilty of *spiritual adultery.* The margin of the ASV has this note: "That is, who break your marriage vow to God"!

When we become Christians, we confess the name of Christ, committing ourselves to Him. Then we are baptized into the church (I Corinthians 12:13), thus becoming a part of Christ's bride. We, in effect, make the most solemn vows to be faithful to Jesus and His cause. Most of us would have little respect for a woman who treated lightly her marriage vows, betraying and being unfaithful to her husband. Being unfaithful to the Lord is cut from the same cloth!

But in what way were James' readers "unfaithful"? By directing their affections to this world instead of to God. Continuing in verse 4: "Know ye not that *the friendship of the world* is enmity with God? Whosoever therefore will be *a friend of the world* is the enemy of God." James places the world on one side and God on the other. The two are diametrically opposed. You cannot love them both. Satan does not mind a divided loyalty, but God does (Matthew 6:24)!

The words "friendship" and "friend" in verse 4 come from the ordinary Greek word for friendship love and affection. In and of itself, this Greek word carries no suggestion of anything that is unsavory, lewd, or immoral. But in this context it is definitely tied with adultery. Which says that one does not become an adulterer or adulteress in a single step. There first is an ill-advised "friendship" that *leads* to the adultery.

To illustrate: A married man works in an office in which there is an attractive woman. They visit; they talk. One day they go to lunch together. He finds her easy to talk to; they can talk without all the responsibilities of married life intruding. They have other lunches together. On a pretty day maybe they take part of the lunch hour to walk through the park. When word reaches his wife, she confronts him with the situation, and he acts offended! "Why we're just friends—just good friends!" he protests—and maybe adds, "What's the matter? Don't you *trust* me?"

If that man is not deliberately unfaithful, he is terribly naive! At some point he passed casual friendship and is flirting with an illicit friendship that can only lead to disaster. He is sinning against his wife and against God!

But is not the same thing true with regards to this world? How many want to flirt with worldliness? How many want to be friendly with the world, not planning to cross over the line! So teenage Christians go to the prom—not to dance but "just to watch." So members of the church of all ages watch R-rated movies, read suggestive books, listen to licentious music—"But it doesn't really affect me," they say. Thus some continue to run around with their old boozing, foul-mouthed, dirty-minded crowd—"they won't influence *me*" is the protest. "What's the matter? Don't you *trust* me?"

Trying to be friendly with the world without being harmed by the world is like a mouse being friendly to a mousetrap, a deer being friendly to a hunter.

A second word that gives insight into the process of

becoming worldly is the word translated "will" in the last part of verse 4. The word in the Greek text refers to an *exercise* of will. This says that worldliness is a result of an action *in the heart.* Occasionally someone that everyone thinks of as a solid Christian seems to change overnight, becoming the most ungodly and worldly of individuals. But the change did not really occur overnight. That person's *mind* was being programmed with worldly thoughts, worldly values, worldly attitudes—for days, weeks, months, perhaps even years—until at last he *resolved* to be the friend of the world.

But the situation is not hopeless. There is . . .

## III. THE CURE FOR WORLDLINESS.
### Verses 5-10.

Some commentators think verse 5 is the most difficult verse in the book of James. I tend to the view that James is here speaking of the Holy Spirit—and therefore that the word "lusteth" (KJV) means "yearns"—and refers to God's Spirit yearning for *us*—for our good. "To envy" would refer to God's reaction to spiritual unfaithfulness. The NIV has this as an alternate reading: "the Spirit he caused to live in us longs jealously." Whether this rendering is correct or not, it *is* true that our God "is a jealous God"(Exodus 20:5), who desires and demands faithfulness on the part of His spiritual bride (II Corinthians 11:2)!

But how can we be faithful? Or if we have been unfaithful, how can we return? The remaining verses give us the *cure* for worldliness. The emphasis in verses 6 through 10 is on GOD and submission to Him:

(1) *Accept the grace of GOD.* Verse 6.

If we had only our own strength on which to rely, the situation would be hopeless. But we have the grace of God to help us meet the challenge. Verse 6 begins: "But he [God] giveth more grace."

It was through grace that we were saved initially (Ephesians 2:8). But the need for God's grace did not cease once we were Christians. Now we need God's grace to *stay* saved (Hebrews 4:16). There are so many ways that God helps us: He has given us His word. We can pray to Him. He has given us meaningful work to do. He has promised His divine protection (I Corinthians 10:13). His Spirit "helps our infirmities" (Romans 8:26). He forgives us when we sin (I John 1:7-9). He has given us "more grace."

As proof that God will give us needed grace, in the last part of verse 6, James quotes from Proverbs 3:34: "God resisteth the proud, but *giveth grace* unto the humble." (Emphasis mine.) Note that we must qualify for that grace. God resists the proud, the self-sufficient, but gives His grace to the humble, the ones who recognize their needs and come to rely on God.

(2) *Be obedient to GOD.* Verse 7.

The result of this humility will be submission to God. Verse 7 begins, "Submit yourselves therefore to God." The word "submit" comes from a military term that means "to stand in rank," to recognize one's rank and act accordingly. In other words, if you are a buck private, don't try to act like a general! God is our spiritual Commander-in-Chief; let us submit to Him, obey Him without question!

An important part of this submission is to decide on whose side we are. James not only says that you must "Submit yourselves therefore to God," he also says, "Resist the devil, and he will flee from you." (Emphasis mine.)

The word "resist" is not a passive word. It refers to "active" opposition. It is another military term that literally means "to set in battle array against." The picture is of the Christian soldier in his place in the army of God, fighting with all his might against the forces of evil.

If you do actively oppose the devil, "he will flee from you" (last of verse 7). Our enemy is formidable, but not irresistible. On television, Geraldine used to say, "The devil made me do it" as though she had no choice. But

James gives you the truth of the matter: "Resist the devil, and he *will* flee from you." (Emphasis mine.)

(3) *Become more like GOD.* Verse 8.

We have noticed military terms in our text. We are not suggesting, however, that there should be the distance between ourselves and God that would normally exist between a private and a five-star general. Rather there is to be a closeness between ourselves and God. James suggests this as he begins verse 8: "Draw nigh [or near] to God, and he will draw nigh to you."

What a promise—God as our close personal companion! But this is conditional upon our first "drawing nigh" to God. How can we draw nigh (or near) to God? A number of things could be mentioned. We need to follow the New Testament with its better hope (Hebrews 7:19). When we fall short, we need to repent (Psalm 34:18). We need to come to God in prayer (Hebrews 4:16). Every possible suggestion, however, can be summed up by saying, *We need to become more like God.*

"Drawing nigh to God" is not a matter of moving east, west, north, or south, or up or down. As far as location is concerned, "he be [is] not far from every one of us" (Acts 17:27). "Drawing nigh to God" rather has to do with becoming more like God so we have things in common, where God's thoughts become ours.

To do this a great many changes have to come into most of our lives. This change is expressed like this in the last part of verse 8: "Cleanse your hands, ye sinners; and purify your hearts, ye double-minded." The need for "clean hands" and "pure hearts" means we need to be clean *inside* and *out.*

How do we cleanse our hands and purify our hearts? By setting our hearts on God and doing His will (Colossians 3:2; I Peter 1:22). For the non-Christian this means he needs to obey *"from the heart* the form of doctrine" (Romans 6:17; emphasis mine) as he is baptized into the death of Christ, buried with Him in baptism, and raised to "walk in newness of life" (Romans 6:3, 4). For the erring child, there is a need for repentance, confession of sins, and prayer to get right with the Lord and His people (Acts 8:22; James 5:16; I John 1:9), followed by the faithful Christian life (Revelation 2:10). For *all* of us, there is the need to strive constantly to be more like God—in thoughts and deeds.

(4) *Humble oneself before GOD.* Verses 9, 10.

Tied so closely with cleansing the hands and purifying the heart is the matter of penitence. It is with this that James closes his discussion of how to cure worldliness: "Be afflicted, and mourn, and weep: let your laughter be turned to mourning, and your joy to heaviness. Humble yourselves in the sight of the Lord, and he shall lift you up" (James 4:9, 10).

Is James against one being happy? No, for in the next chapter he says, "Is any merry? let him sing psalms" (James 5:13). What then is James saying? He is making the same point Ecclesiastes 3:4 makes: There is "a time to weep, and a time to laugh."

I enjoy a good laugh as much as anyone. But sometimes it is not the time to laugh; it is the time to weep. When is the time to weep? When there is sin in the life. When there is sin in the world. When there is sin in the church.

Sin is no laughing matter. When sin runs rampant in our country, our hearts should be grieved. When sin is tolerated in the church, our hearts should be enraged. When sin is in our lives, our hearts should be broken.

And if we *will* thus sorrow for sin? James says: "Humble yourselves in the sight of the Lord, and he shall lift thee up." "He shall lift thee up" in the joy of forgiveness, with new strength and courage, in renewed service.

As we close this chapter we do so with the prayer, "Help us to imbibe the spirit of Jesus—that peace might reign, that we might not be worldly people, that God will ever be exalted."

## FOR DISCUSSION

1. Discuss the basic problem of "the church and the world" (John 17:11, 14).
2. Discuss the Biblical concept of "worldliness." Which of the following would be included in this word: gambling, dancing, "drinking," forsaking worship for personal reasons, seeing that our children get their public school lessons but not their Bible school lessons, being more concerned about paying bills than in going to heaven? Note Matthew 13:22.
3. Discuss the battle all of us must fight ("that war in your members"; see also Romans 7:23cf.; Galatians 5:17; I Peter 2:11).
4. Lust can be defined as "unlawful" desire. What's the difference between lawful and unlawful desire?
5. Verse 2 mentions that these were killing others. Is it possible that *we* could be guilty of this sin (see Matthew 5:22; I John 3:15)?
6. Compare the sins of physical and spiritual adultery.
7. If time permits, note some of the possible meanings of verse 5. Should "spirit" have a capital "S"? What "scripture" is referred to?
8. What does the indwelling Spirit do for us?
9. Does James believe in a personal devil (verse 7)? Can the devil "possess" a person against that person's will?
10. Does verse 9 mean that Christians should never be happy? However is there "a time" to weep (Matthew 5:4; II Corinthians 7:10)?

# WHOM ARE YOU CALLING AN ATHEIST?!

*James 4:11-17*

When you hear the word "atheist," of whom do you think? The local town character who likes to shock people by saying there is no God? A mild-mannered college professor telling his students that the concept of God is outmoded and outdated? Or Madeline O'Hair and her campaign to make America a godless nation? All of these characterizations of the atheist may be true, but for right now let's think about a different kind of atheist.

If I were to ask all who are reading this book who are atheists to hold up their hands, I doubt that many hands would go up. People who believe there is no God seldom read books like this. But having said that, let me suggest that it is possible that there are many readers who are atheists of a certain type—*practical atheists*. By "practical atheists," I refer to *those who LIVE as though there is no God*. If pressed on the matter, they would acknowledge that there is a God, but when one considers their lives, it is obvious that God is not a major factor in their thinking or actions. God is *left out* of their lives.

The theme of "leaving God out" is the key thought that ties James 4:11-17 together. James speaks of leaving God out in at least three ways:

# I. LEAVING GOD OUT OF OUR SPEECH.
## Verses 11, 12.

The problem of misusing the tongue is so prevalent that James has to say one more thing about it: "Speak not evil one of another, brethren. He that speaketh evil of his brother, and judgeth his brother, speaketh evil of the law, and judgeth the law. . . ." (verse 11).

They were speaking "*evil* one of another." The NIV has the right idea when it has, "Brothers, do not *slander* one another." "Slander" refers to defamation of character. It differs from gossip in that it is a *deliberate* attempt to malign another. And, shame of shames, they slandered their fellow Christians. We should not slander anyone, but to slander a brother in Christ is an abominable thing!

How we would like to think that this was an uncommon thing—but it was not and is not. One individual said, "I say it as a fact, that if all men knew what others say of them, there would not be four friends in the world."

But these were not only guilty of slander; they were also guilty of judging their brethren (verse 11). James ties these two sins together. What is the "judging" that James condemns? The best way to describe it is to call it "*misjudging.*" These are some of the features of the judgment condemned in the Bible: (1) Making a judgment from the wrong motives. (2) Making a hasty judgment. (3) Making a judgment from partial or incorrect evidence. (4) Putting the worst possible construction on the facts in the case. (5) Making a judgment regarding the *motives* of the one judged. (6) Being overly harsh in our judgment.

But, we get to our theme as James convicts these brethren not only of slander and misjudging their brethren, but also of *trying to replace God by their actions.* He says this in an unusual way: "He that speaketh evil of his brother, and judgeth his brother, *speaketh evil of the law, and judgeth the law*" (verse 11).

The words "speaketh evil" are used of both the brother and the law. James says that the one who slanders his brother is, in reality, slandering the law! The "law" spoken of here is the same law we've seen throughout our study of the book—"the perfect law of liberty" (James 1:25), "the royal law" (James 2:8), in other words the law of Christ. And what does that law say about the matters of slander and judging? In chapter 2, verse 8, James defines "the royal law" as "Thou shalt love thy neighbor as thyself." Is loving your neighbor compatible with speaking evil of him? No. So if you deliberately slander and misjudge your brother, by your words and actions you are implying that the law to love your brother is not a good and necessary law. You have made a decision, a judgment, about the law. You are indicating that there is no need to obey this law (or, for that matter, any law).

James then notes the logical conclusion of such an action: "But if thou judge the law, thou art not a doer of the law, but a judge" (end of verse 11). Man is to be a law-doer, not a lawgiver (James 1:22). But the one who speaks evil of and slanders another, judging that one's motives and intentions, has set himself up as God. He is saying, "*I* have a right to speak thusly about another. *I* have a right to judge. *I* know all there is to know."

What a temptation it is to so act! But is this right? Listen to James' final word on this subject: "There is one lawgiver, who is able to save and to destroy: who art thou that judgest another?" (verse 12).

This one lawgiver who is able to save and destroy is God (Matthew 10:28; see also Matthew 28:18; Matthew 25). The point is that there is only one *and it is not us*. So James closes this section, "Who art thou that judgest another?" In today's terminology: "Who do you think you are anyway?!"

## II. LEAVING GOD OUT OF OUR PLANNING.
## Verses 13-16.

James' second illustration is in the matter of leaving God out of our *planning*. The imagery used by James would have been very familiar to his Jewish readers:

"Go to now, ye that say, Today or tomorrow we will go into such a city, and continue there a year, and buy and sell, and get gain: whereas ye know not what shall be on the morrow. For what is your life? It is even a vapour, that appeareth for a little time, and then vanisheth away. For that ye ought to say, If the Lord will, we shall live, and do this, or that. But now ye rejoice in your boastings: all such rejoicing is evil" (James 4:13-16).

Prior to the captivity, the Jews had basically been an agricultural people. As they were scattered, they had to adapt or die. Many turned to trading and discovered an aptitude for it. I have heard many disparaging remarks about the Jews as businessmen, but the Jews' ability in this field is a tribute to their tenacity for life. The history of man is full of the stories of people that refused to face change, so they disappeared from the face of the earth.

The Jews became so proficient at this work that, by the time of James, they were actually invited to countries to help the economy. In our text James pictures some who have heard of an attractive business opportunity—either by invitation or because they had good sources of information.

When James speaks of these as "ye that *say*" in verse 13, he is not implying that they were just full of talk. The word "say" is translated from a Greek word that means "to speak . . . as a result of *sound reasoning* and *careful planning*." Notice how careful their planning was: They had planned the time to start, the place to trade, how long the venture would last, their activity, and the results.

"So what's the problem?" someone asks. "Isn't this a good example of the free-enterprise system?" What *is* the problem with the scene pictured in verse 13?

Is James condemning trading or being a *businessman?* No, in and of itself there is nothing wrong with engaging in business (Proverbs 22:29). Is James saying there is something wrong with *making a profit?* No, there's nothing wrong with making a profit as long as it is reasonable and as long as one does not hurt others. Is James perhaps saying that it is wrong to *plan ahead?* No, Ephesians 5:16 says we need to "redeem the time" (making the most of it—RSV) and we can't do that if we do not plan ahead.

If James is not speaking against such things, what *is* he speaking against? *He is speaking against leaving GOD out of our planning.* Look again at the words of verse 13. Not a word about God. No indication at all that they were even slightly interested in what GOD might think about their plans.

In the next few verses James shows the foolishness of those who boldly said, "We will do this or that," without considering the will of God:

(1) *They were foolish because they did not take into account the uncertainty of life.* "Whereas ye know not what shall be on the morrow" (verse 14a). They planned confidently for a *year*, but in actuality they did not even know what *the next day* might bring.

They planned to start "today or tomorrow"—but they might get sick. They planned to go into a certain city—but war might disrupt travel. They planned to stay a year—but the market might collapse within a year. They planned to buy and sell and get gain—but the government might not allow them to trade, or thieves might steal their goods or their profits.

One thing that might happen to disrupt all their carefully laid plans was *death*—which brings us to James' next point:

(2) *They were foolish because they did not take into account the brevity of life.*

In the middle of verse 14, James asks one of the most thought-provoking questions that could be asked: "For what is your life?" What answer would *you* give to that question? Many answers might be given, both negative and positive, but the point that James wants to emphasize is that it is a very *short* period of time. "It is even a vapour, that appeareth for a little time, and then vanisheth away" (verse 14b). Many illustrations are used through the Bible to stress how quickly life passes (Job 7:6, 9; 8:9; Matthew 6:30; I Peter 1:24). But none is more graphic than the figure used by James. I don't know what vapor James had in mind—smoke, fog, a cloud, steam rising from a boiling pot. But whatever the type of vapor considered, it is *so quickly gone.*

Even if one lives to a ripe old age, life is so short. But James seems to be stressing that we cannot even count on getting old. A tiny blood clot can dislodge somewhere in the body, make its way through a vein until it hits the heart, and life is over. Your car can hit an icy spot on the highway, go out of control, and you have gone to meet your Maker.

The rich merchants were thinking in terms of 365 days of trading, but James says, You cannot even be sure of *tomorrow.*

(3) *They were foolish because they did not take into account THE WILL OF GOD.* In verse 15 James says, "For that ye ought to say, *If the Lord will,* we shall live, and do this, or that."

Notice the two things qualified by the phrase, "If the Lord will": "If the Lord will, we shall *live*"—our lives will be extended. And "if the Lord will, we shall . . . do this or that"—we shall be able to carry out our plans. Let it be stressed that planning ahead is not discouraged here, *as long as one understands that all plans are subject to the will of God!*

The phrase "If the Lord will" indicates several things about the person who says it: It indicates that the person believes in God, that he believes God is in control, and, most importantly, it indicates that he believes that *his life* needs to be controlled by God! It was a phrase and concept constantly on the lips of Paul and other New Testament Christians (Acts 18:21; 21:14; Romans 1:10; 15:32; I

Corinthians 4:19; 16:7).

Through our lives we must make hundreds of decisions: Where we are going to live, where we are going to work, how we are going to use our time, where we are going to worship and serve the Lord, where our children will go to school, and so on. As we make those decisions, what considerations are at the top of the list? Convenience? Money? The possibility for promotion? Personal preference? Or is *the will of God* at the top of the list?!

(4) *They were foolish because they were proud of themselves and their abilities.*

James says, "But now ye rejoice in your boastings: all such rejoicing is evil" (verse 16). Instead of trusting in God and instead of submitting to His will, they were proud of what *they* had done in the past and boasted of what *they* planned to do in the future. It is permissible to be proud of *some* things (Hebrews 3:6; II Corinthians 7:4; 10:17; II Thessalonians 1:4). But it is a sin to be proud of one's own accomplishments, failing to give God the glory.

Again we have the message given in our last lesson: "*Humble* yourselves in the sight of the Lord, and he shall lift you up" (James 4:11; emphasis mine). Instead of exalting self, we need to exalt God in all things—especially as we plan and make decisions.

## III. LEAVING GOD OUT OF OUR ACTIVITIES. Verse 17.

In chapter 4, verse 17, James makes one of the great sweeping statements of the Bible with far-reaching application: "Therefore to him that knoweth to do good, and doeth it not, to him it is sin." Those of whom James writes had both the opportunity to learn and had applied themselves to study. They *knew* what was right and what was wrong. They even knew they should *do* good. But there they stopped. They did not do what they knew to do. And in that failure to do, they sinned.

Perhaps I should pause to stress that this passage is *not* teaching that ignorance justifies. The Bible is clear on the point that ignorance alone does not excuse (I Timothy 1:13, 15; Acts 17:30; Romans 3:23; 6:23).

What *is* the point James is making? James is pointing out the seriousness of deliberate, willful sin! Think about it. Here is an individual who knows there is an all-powerful God who has made everything, an all-powerful God before whom he must stand to give an account someday. Further this individual *knows* what this God has asked him to do—there is no question in his mind as to what he should do. And then this individual coolly, deliberately, and disdainfully refuses to do what he knows the God of the universe has told him to do! The implications of this willful disobedience are enough to send shivers up the spine (Hebrews 10:26-31)!

There is another point to be made from James' statement: James says nothing here about doing what is *wrong*; he only speaks of failing to do what is right—what the pioneer preachers called "the sin of omission."

I fear that there are some who think their relationship with God rests entirely upon their leaving out of their lives things that are bad, never realizing that it is also sin to fail to include in their lives those things that are good. Guy N. Woods, noted gospel preacher who first trained as a lawyer, thinks he could successfully defend the individual spoken of in James 4:17 if the jury was composed of twelve typical members of the church. I would point out, says Woods, that this man did not drink, did not gamble, did not run around on his wife, did not cheat on his income tax, and did not beat up on small children. I do not doubt, concludes Woods, that I could get a verdict of "not guilty"! . . . But the man *was* guilty—guilty of failing to do what was *right*.

Do you *know* you should be studying the Bible more (II Timothy 2:15)—but are not doing it? That's sin! Do you *know* you should be spending more time in prayer and meditation (Psalm 1:2)—but are doing nothing about it? That's sin! Do you *know* you should be helping others (Galatians 6:10)—but are not? That's sin! Do you *know* you should be using your talents in the service of God (I Corinthians 15:58)—but are not? That's sin! Do you *know* you should be teaching others and sharing your faith (Matthew 28:19)—but are failing to do so? *That's sin!*

With these three illustrations of "leaving God out," we have given a fairly comprehensive view of "practical atheism": Leaving God out of our speech, leaving God out of our planning, leaving God out of our activities, *i.e.*, out of our (1) words, (2) thoughts, and (3) deeds! Our prayer is that each of us will not merely give lip service to the existence of God, but will in *every* way (in word, in thought, in deed) acknowledge His presence and our daily dependence upon Him.

## FOR DISCUSSION

1. Is "speaking evil" about others still a common sin today? *Why* is this such a common sin? What psychological needs are satisfied by dragging down others? But does this make it right?
2. Could there be slander-speakers without slander-hearers? (II John 11). What should we do if we are in a group where someone is "evil-spoken-of"?
3. Discuss the sin of judging (Matthew 7:1, 2): What is judging? Are all judgments the judging that is condemned (Matthew 7:6; James 5:19, 20; John 7:24)? Why do people judge? What are the results of judging? Etc.
4. Discuss the problems of the Christian businessman today.
5. Discuss the need for planning ahead—and how it can be done without leaving God out.
6. What are some possible answers to the question "What is your life?"
7. Is life short (Job 14:1, 2)? How should the realization of this

make us act (Proverbs 27:1)? What were the mistakes of the Rich Fool (Luke 12:16-21)?

8. Do we have to *say* "if the Lord wills" every time we speak of the future? Would there be value in our saying these words much more than we do (Luke 22:42)?

9. Someone has said that we do not bring the Lord into our decisions until *after* we make them—and then we ask the Lord to *bless* those decisions. Do you think this is true?

10. Is the "sin of omission" as bad as the "sin of commission"? Why do you suppose many of us *know* what we should do, and do not do it?

# BEWARE OF THE DANGERS OF RICHES!

*James 5:1-6*

God is interested in *everything* concerning our money. He is interested in how much we get and how we get it. He is interested in the part we spend and the part we save. He is interested in the part we give and the part we keep for ourselves. This point is made in our text: James 5:1-6. Every blessing from God brings a corresponding responsibility. We are but stewards of all we possess. As we strive to be good stewards, our text would warn us of some dangers of which to beware:

## I. THE DANGER OF TRUSTING IN RICHES.
## Verse 1.

James never sounds more like an Old Testament prophet than when he says: "Go to now, ye rich men, weep and howl for your miseries that shall come upon you" (verse 1).

In context the "rich men" addressed are probably the rich Jewish landowners in Judea. In most of the world common labor was done by slaves. Palestine was unique in that farm labor was still done by hired workers. Since verse 4 refers to hired workers, most authorities are agreed that the setting is that of the area around Jerusalem where James made his home. As we will notice later, these were non-

Christian Jews who hated and oppressed Christians, most of whom were poor.

James says to these wicked rich, "Weep and howl for your miseries that shall come upon you." Only a few years after James wrote this book, Jerusalem was destroyed by the Roman army. At that time the wealthy Sadducees lost all their wealth and over one million were ruthlessly murdered. But, if one missed that, there was the Day of Judgment. Terrible things were coming upon those who trusted in their riches!

"So James wrote to tell the rich folks of the Day of the Judgment awaiting them, so what? Nothing of what he says has anything to do with us." Are you sure?

By the standards of the world as a whole most of us are *rich*. For instance the average income in China is about $300 a year; how much did *we* make last year? My daughter visited Indonesia a few months ago. She stayed with a well-to-do family that had servants to perform many manual tasks. One servant took their clothes to a nearby stream and pounded them clean on the rocks. Another servant warmed water and filled a tub when someone wanted to bathe. When they wanted to go from place to place, they hired someone to pull them. Someone says, "I wish I could have servants like that." We do! Only we call them the washing machine, the hot-water heater, and the automobile. I repeat, most of us are *rich*.

And we can trust in money as surely as any Jewish landowner ever did! "We have 'In God We Trust' engraved on our coins, but 'Me First' engraved on our hearts." People think, if I could only have enough money, I would be happy.

But James declares to us an important truth: Money is no assurance of happiness. The rich have the burden of care in getting riches, the burden of anxiety in keeping riches, the burden of temptation in using riches, the burden of guilt in abusing riches. The rich have problems just like anyone else. And the rich who *trust* in their riches, instead of in God

(I Timothy 6:17), will howl and shriek throughout eternity.

## II. THE DANGER OF HOARDING RICHES.
### Verses 2, 3.

One misery that would come upon the ungodly rich would be the ease with which the treasures in which they trusted could be destroyed: "Your riches are corrupted, and your garments are moth-eaten. Your gold and silver is cankered" (verses 2, 3).

In those days, one's wealth was not tied up in pieces of paper stored in a vault. Rather one's riches were represented in tangible things. There were three basic types of wealth: The produce of the earth such as grain and vegetable oil, cloth items such as wearing apparel, and precious jewels and metals. All three are represented in these verses.

James first says, "Your riches are corrupted." "Corrupted" refers to decaying or rotting. The reference is to grain and other materials that can rot. Then he says, "Your garments are moth-eaten." Part of their wealth was in wearing apparel, but mothballs had not yet been invented.

Finally he says, "Your gold and silver is cankered." Some translations have "rusted" here. But the process of oxidation is not primarily on the mind of James. The original literally says "your gold and silver have *rusted through*," i.e., they are destroyed. Even though precious metals do not rot and cannot be eaten by insects, this form of wealth is also temporary. Thieves can steal them (Matthew 6:19) or they can lose their value.

So James makes the point that riches are impermanent and are rapidly departing. But he *primarily* is concerned with the fact that the rich did not *use* their riches for the benefit of mankind. While people around them were hungry, the rich had food in storage that was rotting. While people were ill-clothed and unprotected from the cold, they had stored garments that were being eaten by the moths. While they were surrounded by the poor, they had silver and gold that was doing no one any good.

So James continues in verse 3: "And the rust of them shall be a witness against you, and shall eat your flesh as it were fire. Ye have heaped treasure together for the last days."

This verse depicts a courtroom scene. Rich men oppressed the Christians and drew them before judgment seats (James 2:6; 5:6). Now these same men will themselves be called into a higher court—and the first witness against them will be "the rust" of their gold and silver, in other words their unused wealth.

There is irony here. These had been "heaping together treasure" for their "last days." They thought their treasures would be their comfort and strength in days to come. Instead their treasures are called to the witness stand to testify *against* them. Their unused treasures condemn them.

The result will be the "miseries" James mentioned earlier. "The rust" that testified will also "eat your flesh as it were fire." The writer pictures the rust as a contagion spreading from the precious metal to the very flesh of the rich. Flesh does not rust, but it can be oxidized in fire, so the rust of their unused wealth is pictured as igniting the very fires of hell.

Are there any lessons here for us? At first glance we might be tempted to say, "no." Maybe there's a small percentage of people who hoard wealth, but most of us don't! If there is anything we do well as a nation and as individuals, it is spend money. We don't keep our money long enough to get dust on it, much less rust.

But think again. And scenes of embarrassing unused and even rotting wealth may come to mind. Like scenes of storage bins full of foodstuffs, paid for by the government, and stored to keep the cost of those commodities at a certain level.

But let's get closer to home. Is it possible that *we* as

individuals have treasures that we selfishly keep to ourselves, without sharing, without using them for the glory of God? Do we have houses that we never use in God's service—houses that do not know the hospitality God desires (Hebrews 13:1)? Do we have cars that we use only for ourselves—cars that could be used to bring others to services? Or to look at the three categories James uses: Is it possible that we as Americans throw away enough food each day to feed much of the hungry of the world? Is it possible that we have enough clothes in our closets to clothe most of the naked of the world? Is it possible that we have possessions we do not even have time to use that could be sold to send men to preach the gospel to a lost and dying world?

In this nation we have been blessed materially above all people who have ever lived upon the earth. But the blessings we have are all temporary. They are all in the process of decay. We must use them for the glory of God and use them NOW. Otherwise the "rust" of them may witness against *us* in the Judgment—and may eat *our* flesh like fire!

### III. THE DANGER OF GAINING RICHES IN THE WRONG WAY.
### Verse 4.

In verse 4 James notes another specific sin of the wicked rich. They not only selfishly withheld their riches from the poor in general, they even withheld wages from their employees: "Behold, the hire of the labourers who have reaped down your fields, which is of you kept back by fraud, crieth: and the cries of them which have reaped are entered into the ears of the Lord of sabaoth."

There are many ways these rich men could have kept back all or part of their laborers' wages. They could have forced them to agree on a substandard wage in the first place. They could have paid them only part of what they agreed upon, perhaps saying that they had not received as much for their crops as they had anticipated. Or perhaps they kept putting off paying the laborers, promising them their wages soon. But whatever their excuse, the text says they were *dishonest* in the dealings; they "kept back" the wages "by fraud."

Such dishonesty went against every law of man and God. The Old Testament had taught that not even a single day should go by without a hired laborer being paid (Deuteronomy 24:14, 15). The poor were so destitute that withholding their pay for even one day could spell disaster. In the New Testament, it is stressed again and again that the laborer is worthy of his hire (Luke 10:7; I Timothy 5:18; etc.).

But what the wicked failed to pay to their farm workers, they would pay for in Judgment. James returns to the courtroom scene: "The hire . . . which is . . . kept back by fraud, crieth: and the cries of them which have reaped are entered into the ears of the Lord of sabaoth." There will be two other witnesses that will testify against these ungodly landowners. The second witness that would take the stand would be the wages they failed to pay. The third witness would be the workers themselves who had been defrauded.

The cries of the defrauded (Deuteronomy 24:15) reached their mark. "The cries . . . are entered into the ears of the Lord of sabaoth." In this scene, the Judge is not a judge who can be swayed by the power of the rich landowners. Rather the Judge is the Lord Himself!

He is here called "the Lord of sabaoth." Not "sabbath," but "sabaoth." The word "sabaoth" means "hosts" and refers to the hosts of heaven—the heavenly bodies, the angels, yea of all creation. The phrase declares Him to be the Commander-in-Chief of the Universe. Those who are being oppressed by the wicked should take heart. Their cries are heard. And they are heard by One infinitely more powerful than those who are mistreating them—One who has the power to correct all wrongs, reward the righteous, and to punish the wicked!

The lesson to us is that God is concerned about how we get our money! I see a philosophy taking over our country that says, "It makes no difference who I hurt just as long as I get ahead." Manipulators of companies work out their mergers and accomplish their take-overs, often with little thought for the number they may put out of work. The liquor industry is concerned about the profit margin, not the multitudes destroyed physically and spiritually because of their product. Publishers, television producers, moviemakers seldom seem to care about the influence of their products as long as these productions make money. And a lack of concern for others is not limited to the rich and powerful. The common man says, "Sue the huge corporations for all you can; they can afford it."

But the Bible teaches us differently. The Bible teaches us to *work* for our money. The Bible teaches us to be more concerned about others than we are about ourselves. The Bible teaches that God is as concerned about how we *make* our money as He is about how we *use* our money.

## IV. THE DANGER OF USING RICHES
## ONLY FOR SELF.
### Verse 5.

In verse 5, James says, "Ye have lived in pleasure on the earth, and been wanton; ye have nourished your hearts, as in a day of slaughter."

See the laborers in their hovels, their faces gaunt from hunger. See the sadness on their faces as they hear their children whimpering in their sleep because they have no food. Imagine them as they go out into the night to escape the sounds of their starving children. But outside, new sounds come to their ears: The sounds of laughter and music coming from the opulent homes of the rich. And on the breeze are the smells of meat cooking and pastries baking. Can you not feel the anger of the poor at this display of plenty when they have nothing?!

The rich oppressed their hired servants, even refusing to pay them a living wage. At the same time *they* "lived in pleasure" and were "wanton." The NIV says that they lived "in luxury and self-indulgence." By living in such a manner, they were guilty of at least two sins: First, they lived useless, indolent, empty lives—contributing nothing to the betterment of mankind. Second, they lived in luxury and therefore lived wasteful lives. And wastefulness is a renouncement of the stewardship placed upon every man by God.

The end result of this self-indulgent life? "Ye have nourished your hearts, as in a day of slaughter." The word "nourished" is translated "fattened" in many of the translations. The picture is that of an animal being fattened in preparation for slaughter.

In western Oklahoma and elsewhere, in order to get top market price, at a certain point in the year the big ranchers take their cattle off the pasture and put them in enormous feedlots. Thousands of head of cattle are crammed into these lots, with little room to move about, and nothing to do but eat. They are given all the food they can eat. It's as close to heaven as a steer ever gets. But every day that goes by, that steer is one day closer to being a steak on someone's dinner table!

These indolent, unproductive rich were stuffing themselves in self-indulgence, thinking they were the only ones who really knew how to live, while all the time they were really already in the chute, being herded to the slaughterhouse!

It hurts to think about how applicable this is to the U.S. We are a country of self-indulgers. Most of us are not highly immoral or criminal; we're just self-indulgent. We are constantly bombarded by Madison Avenue concerning all these things we really *need* to have, really *must* have, and so we rush out and buy, buy, buy—all for self, all for our own comfort, our own gratification. And that reference to being fattened for slaughter comes too close for comfort. As a whole we are probably the most overweight nation who ever existed.

How we need the viewpoint of Jesus who said, "The Son of man came not to be ministered unto, but to minister, and to give his life a ransom for many" (Matthew 20:28)! If we use our blessings only for ourselves, like those James speaks of, *we* may be fattening our own hearts for a day of slaughter.

## V. THE DANGER OF MISUSING THE POWER OF RICHES.
## Verse 6.

James concludes his condemnation of the ungodly rich: "Ye have condemned and killed the just; and he doth not resist you" (James 5:6).

The word "condemned" is a legal term. It refers to a legal sentence being handed down—a sentence of death. In context it refers to a miscarriage of justice, for the one thus sentenced to death is referred to as a "just" man. Further this just man is defenseless, unable to resist the rich and powerful. The picture is that of ruthless men using their wealth to manipulate the courts to their own ends—even to killing innocent men if it served their purposes.

In the original text, "the just" is in the singular and in some translations is rendered "the just one." Many are convinced that this can only refer to Jesus (Acts 3:14; 7:52; 22:14; I John 2:1; I Peter 2:21-23; Isaiah 53:7). Others think this refers to Jesus as representative of all Christians; that which is done to His followers is done to Him (Matthew 25:40). Many modern translators feel that this refers to *any* just man, especially the poor who would be incapable of resistance. They frequently translate the phrase "just *men.*" The point being made is the *unfairness* of the ungodly rich. They used their power and influence to condemn and kill *any* righteous person who opposed them.

The rich felt they were above the law, but ultimately *they* would be hauled into court (verse 4)—the Court of Eternal Judgment, the court from which there was no appeal. As they had done, so it would be done to them. The next verse begins: "Be patient therefore, brethren, unto the coming of the Lord" (James 5:7). Things may look black, but the Lord *will* return; He will make things right!

Again this lesson to us is to be so careful of how we use our blessings. If God sees fit to bless us with material things, this does not make us more important nor give to us any special privileges. It rather places upon us a heavier responsibility to use those blessings in a way to bless the world and to glorify the One who so blessed us.

May God help us to learn to use—not misuse—the great blessings that are ours!

## FOR DISCUSSION

1. As time permits, discuss the vital theme of "The Christian and His Money." What about this attitude: "I give what I can and what I do with what's left is *my* business"? Especially note the Biblical teaching on stewardship.
2. Does James condemn being rich *per se* (James 1:9, 10)? Does the Bible mention any rich men who were godly? Are there, however, so many problems connected with being rich that it can be said that it is *almost* impossible for the rich to be saved (Luke 8:24cf.; 18:25cf.; I Timothy 6:9, 10cf.)?
3. Is it still a real temptation to trust in riches? Can you think of any examples in today's society? Note I Timothy 6:17.
4. What is the difference, if any, between *hoarding* and *saving?*
5. Discuss passages like I Timothy 6:9, 10, 17-19; Matthew 6:19-21 that tell how the rich can be saved.
6. How does verse 4 of our text show that the Bible is just as concerned about employees as it is about employers? Does the Bible speak to *both* capital and labor (Colossians 3:22, 23; 4:1)? Would Matthew 7:12 be helpful in employer-

employee relationships?

7. Give some examples of the philosophy: "I don't care whom I hurt as long as I get what I have coming to me."
8. Discuss the problem of self-indulgence. Note Amos 6:1, 4-6; I Timothy 5:6.
9. Would James himself later serve to illustrate verse 6? See the first lesson to see how James "the Just" died.
10. Has the injustice pictured by James in verse 6 vanished from the earth? What comfort does verse 7 give?

# GIVE ME PATIENCE — RIGHT NOW!

*James 5:7-12*

The emphasis in James 5:7-12 is on *patience*—an extremely important subject. Frankly, patience is not our greatest virtue. Back in the 1920s, one writer said concerning America, "It is on the move—and impatient with delay." Sixty-plus years later we are still impatient with delay. We buy dinners that can be ready in minutes. We want instant potatoes, instant oatmeal, instant rice. Our regular oven is too slow, so we get a microwave. We put transistors in our television sets so we don't have to wait for our sets to warm up before we can see the program. We must have freeways with no stop lights that would slow us down. Our attitude is well expressed in the familiar story of the man who prayed, "Lord, give me patience—and give it to me right now!"

But what is this thing called "patience"? The dictionary says that the primary meaning is "the quality or habit of enduring without complaint." Someone has defined it as "the ability to idle your motor when you feel like stripping your gears." This quality is generally translated in the KJV as "longsuffering." In the passage under discussion, however, it is translated as "patient" or "patience" four times (verses 7, 8, 10). The word in the original literally means to be "long-tempered." "Long-tempered" is the opposite of "*short*-tempered"!

However in verse 11 James twice uses the word usually translated "patient" in the KJV—the word that means "steadfast endurance." This refers to the ability to keep going without quitting, even under duress. James uses the two terms interchangeably, indicating that the "patience" he has in mind *combines* the qualities of the two Greek words used: It is a patience that does not quit; it is also a patience that maintains a good attitude! In our text James has at least four things to say to us concerning patience:

## I. BE PATIENT IN YOUR WORK.
## Verses 7, 8.

Verses 1 through 6 of James 5 emphasized that the wicked who persecuted Christians *would* be punished; now James tells Christians that this will happen when Christ returns: "Be patient therefore, brethren, unto the coming of the Lord" (verse 7).

James stresses that his readers should not be wasting their time being overly concerned about whether their persecutors would be punished or not. That was God's business, not theirs (Romans 12:19). They could take comfort in the fact that Christ was returning to settle all such matters. This being the case, they should not allow themselves to be distracted by thoughts of retribution, but should rather settle down and become absorbed in the work God had given them to do.

James uses the farmer as an illustration of the patience his readers need: "Behold, the husbandman waiteth for the precious fruit of the earth, and hath long patience for it, until he receive the early and latter rain" (verse 7).

If there is any quality a farmer must possess, it is patience. Immediately after one harvest, he must begin preparation for the next harvest by plowing, cultivating, fertilizing. He then waits for the early rain—the rain in the fall that raises the water level and allows the seed to be planted. In the winter there are a hundred things that must be done: work on equipment, fences, and buildings. In springtime he waits for the latter rain—the rain that either triggers the germination or causes the young plants to grow. If the first seed sown comes up, he must keep the growing crop cultivated, free of weeds, and safe from destructive animals and insects. If the first seeds sown do not come up, he quickly replants, praying that he is not too late.

By summertime, the farmer's financial resources are usually depleted. The plants grow so slowly but there is no way he can hurry the growing process. He can only do what he can to protect the growing crop—and "wait" and have "long patience."

What enables him to have such patience? Several things help: He knows that this is the procedure that must be followed to get a crop. He knows that being impatient won't hurry the process. He could fret for eleven months, and it would still take the same length of time for the crop to grow. But most importantly, he is willing to be patient because of the end result of his patient labor. He waits "for the precious fruit of the earth." The hope of harvest makes it all worthwhile.

So James says in verse 8: "Be ye also patient." (Emphasis mine.) Be patient as the farmer is. "Stablish your hearts." The ASV has "establish" your hearts. The NASB has "strengthen" your hearts. Don't let persecution and oppression get you down; take heart! Why? "For the coming of the Lord draweth nigh." *Your* harvest time is almost here—the time when the Lord shall reward the faithful and punish the persecutors. If the farmer waits patiently because of the *possibility* of a harvest, how much more patient *you* should be, for with the Lord there are no crop failures; your reward is *sure!*

When James said,"The coming of the Lord draweth nigh," he was not trying to set the time of Christ's return—as something that was going to happen in the next few years. James and others understood that no man knows the time

(Matthew 24:42) and that the Second Coming will come unexpectedly (I Thessalonians 5:2). Why then did he speak of the Second Coming as "nigh" or near? Because we must always think of Christ's coming as something (1) that is sure and (2) that can occur at any moment. The mother warns the child, "You had better behave; Daddy is coming," or comforts the child with the words, "Daddy will be here before long." So, James says in effect, "Be patient, take heart, the Lord really is coming!"

There are many lessons for us in these two verses, but one of the most important is the need to be patient in our *work* for the Lord. The farmer waited for harvest, but he did not wait with folded hands. He waited with plow in hand, with seed in hand, with tools in hand, with hoe in hand. While he waited, he worked.

Some of us spiritually-speaking have no taste for the drawn-out work of the farmer. We want instant results. We start programs with great enthusiasm—but if we do not turn the world upside down overnight, we get impatient and quit. James would say to us: The Lord is coming. All will turn out all right. This is sure! So keep going, be patient, don't quit. Realize that good works take time, so don't get discouraged. Harvest time will make it all worthwhile!

## II. BE PATIENT WITH EACH OTHER.
## Verse 9.

Have you ever noticed this common phenomenon: When we get frustrated or angry or we are hurt by others, we tend to take it out on those nearest and dearest to us? This is illogical, but so common! This seems to be the problem James addresses in verse 9. His readers were being oppressed and persecuted by non-Christians. So what did they do? They started fussing and finding fault with fellow Christians! So James says, "Grudge not one against another, brethren, lest ye be condemned: behold, the judge standeth before the door" (James 5:9).

The word translated "grudge" in the KJV literally means "to groan." It is a word that refers to outward expression rather than suffering silently. The ASV translates it "murmur." The NASB has "complain." There are at least three sins involved here: First is the sin of being a groaner, murmurer, complainer. Some of us tend to be quarrelsome people, quick to take offense, and quick to find fault (note I Corinthians 10:10).

Second is the sin of murmuring against *a brother*. James says,"Grudge not *one against another, brethren*." The ones being attacked were brethren in Christ, those in the family of God, those "for whom Christ died" (I Corinthians 8:11)! To return to the illustration of the farmer: How foolish that farmer would be if he said, "It is so long until harvest. So I think I'll have a fight with my wife," or "Rather than spend my time working while I'm waiting for the crop to mature, I'll spend my time complaining about my neighbors." In those days, a farmer was dependent upon family and neighbors for survival. It was almost impossible to make it without friends. This is so in the spiritual vineyard of God—the kingdom, the church: *We need each other*. How foolish to murmur and complain about each other!

Finally, there is the sin of murmuring against a brother *before others*. This is implied in the passage. As a rule, those who develop a critical and fault-finding spirit end up being careless about those to whom they complain—even when that "murmuring" can only harm the cause of Christ! James says to his readers, Don't do this! Do not murmur against one another, "lest ye be *condemned*."

Again James reminds them that the Lord is coming: "Behold, the judge standeth before the door" (verse 9). This is an obvious reference to Jesus. "Standing before the door" indicates that He is ready to come in. James made the point in the two previous verses that Jesus was returning to judge the wicked unbelievers, but his readers should not think they were exempt from judgment. The Lord *could* return to punish *them* for wrong attitudes toward, and wrong treatment of, their fellow Christians!

Some self-examination is in order here. What *is* our attitude toward other members of the church? *Do* we tend to be hypercritical? Do we complain about the elders, the preacher, or any other members? Have we developed the habit of grumbling or complaining? If we find we have a problem here, here are several suggestions: (1) Let us learn to *pray* for those whom we criticize. It is hard to murmur and pray at the same time. (2) Instead of complaining about someone, let us learn to *go* to that one to discuss the problem (Matthew 5:22-24). (3) Instead of talking about others, let us learn to keep our mouths shut. "If you can't say something good, don't say anything at all!" (4) Let us learn to *love* each other. Love puts the best possible construction on a man's actions (I Corinthians 13:7). Love covers a "multitude of sins" (I Peter 4:8). We should never excuse or condone sin, but how many times it would help if we had more love and understanding.


## III. BE PATIENT IN THE MIDST OF TRIALS.
### Verses 10, 11.

James now goes to the heart of what was bothering his readers—the problems they had to endure even though they were doing the best they could (James 5:10, 11).

Throughout the years, the problem of suffering has perplexed men. One of the most puzzling aspects of the problem has been, why do *good* men suffer? Not infrequently men have asked that question from a personal viewpoint: Why do *I* suffer, why do I have all these problems, when I am doing my best to be what God wants me to be?

But the most puzzling aspect of all, to those who are trying to be and do good, has been, Why do I suffer *for doing good?* A young person determines that he will be pure when he is married, and his buddies make fun of him—perhaps even call him "gay." An employee refuses to go along with the unethical practices of his employers and is passed over for promotion. A Christian woman brings Biblical teaching into a neighborhood discussion on the latest divorce, and receives frosty looks from the others present. And these cry out, "But I was trying to do what was *right!* Why should I suffer for that?!"

No more appropriate example of this paradox could have been chosen by James than that which he uses: The prophets—men like Elijah, Elisha, Jeremiah, Daniel, Ezekiel. These were men, James says, who spoke "in the name of the Lord" (verse 10). They were God's personal spokesmen. But they still suffered affliction! As a group, they were probably the most persecuted men in history (note Hebrews 11:37, 38). It is important for us to realize that if we try to do right, we *will* have trials. *Satan* will see to that. "All that will live godly in Christ Jesus *shall* suffer persecution" (II Timothy 3:12; emphasis mine). The prophets are vivid proof of this.

But James does not merely hold up the prophets as examples of "suffering affliction" for doing what is right, but also examples "*of patience.*" And, in these two verses, James blends the two aspects of patience—patient endurance and endurance with the right attitude.

As a rule the prophets had a good attitude; they did not moan and groan about their lot in life. Then James begins verse 11: "Behold, we count them happy [or blessed] which *endure.*" (Emphasis mine.) The prophets did not give up. They were persecuted for doing what was right. They were mistreated for speaking for God. But they didn't get discouraged and quit. They stayed true to the Lord, even though that commitment cost them dearly.

There are many lessons for us: If we try to do right, we will have persecution. When that persecution comes, we should try to maintain a good, positive attitude. When that persecution comes, we need to resolve to remain faithful to the Lord, no matter what. However, one of the most important lessons is that we *can* endure, we *can* remain faithful to the Lord no matter what comes. The prophets did; so can we. Then, we, too, can be counted as blessed of the Lord!

Now James goes from the general example of the prophets to a specific example, "the patience of *Job*."

The book of Job is the original treatise on the problem of suffering, the first effort to struggle with the question of why good men have bad problems. Job was "a perfect and upright man, one that feared God, and escheweth [turned away from] evil" (Job 1:8). But he still lost all his physical possessions, all of his children were killed, he contracted the most excruciating of diseases, and, on top of it all, family and friends tormented him with accusations. If any man ever had good reason to quit, to forsake the Lord, it was Job. But he did not. He didn't understand why all these things were happening to him, but he declared that he was on God's side and there he would stay (Job 1:21; 13:15)!

Because Job tenaciously clung to the Lord, he can be counted as happy and blessed. "Ye . . . have seen the end of the Lord," says James, "that the Lord is very pitiful [full of pity], and of tender mercy" (verse 11). The book of Job can be divided into three parts: Job's distress (chapters 1-3), Job's defense (chapters 4-31), but finally Job's deliverance (chapters 38-42). I like happy endings. Many modern novels no longer have happy endings, but the book of Job does (42:12, 13, 16).

Be patient. Endure to the end. Maybe things will go well with you in this life and maybe they won't. But one thing we can be *sure* of. When at last we make it to that home of the soul, heaven itself, *there* we shall receive that grand welcome from the Lord Himself (Matthew 25:21)!

# IV. BE PATIENT IN YOUR SPEECH.
## Verse 12.

At first glance one might think that James has changed the subject in verse 12, but then we see that the verse starts with the word "but," which ties it in with the verses before—and, therefore, with the general subject of patience: "But above all things, my brethren, swear not, neither by heaven, neither by the earth, neither by any other oath: but let your yea be yea; and your nay, nay; lest ye fall into condemnation" (James 5:12).

What does all this have to do with the subject of patience? Just this: If we are impatient, invariably that impatience will find expression in our *words*. We will complain and criticize (verse 9). Our words will become harsh, condemning, flamboyant, exaggerated, inappropriate. It is this tendency, common to us all, that James addresses.

The specific expression of impatience that James deals with is swearing. What we generally refer to as swearing is profanity, while the swearing mentioned here refers to taking an oath. In the light of the context, it probably refers to invoking a curse upon those who were persecuting them. The two types of swearing are so interrelated, that I will make no effort to distinguish between them. I believe James condemns *both* in the last part of the verse. Whether it is swearing, profanity, cursing, or giving an oath, James says, don't do it!

There is a very widely-accepted philosophy today that it would be better if one did not curse, but in situations of great stress and excitement, cursing is to be expected and even condoned. If you tend to feel this way, for a moment think of the stress these Christians were under. They were being persecuted unbearably. They were starving while their persecutors were living in luxury. They were being cheated. They were being treated unjustly in the courts. As a result some had been provoked into calling down curses upon their persecutors. If anyone could ever be excused for swearing with an oath, surely it was these. But listen carefully to James: "*Swear not,* . . . lest ye fall into condemnation"!

The writer's Jewish readers should have known this type of thing was wrong. Starting with commandment number four ("Thou shalt not take the name of the Lord thy God in vain"), the Old Testament had severely condemned this type of speech. But the Jews had come up with a dodge; they thought as long as they did not use the name of God, their oaths really did not matter. So James tells them, "Swear not, neither by heaven, neither by the earth." And to cover every possibility, he adds, "neither by *any other* oath."

Today folks still have their dodges to try to excuse their vulgar language. "I do it without thinking" (see Matthew 12:34). "Where I work (or go to school) everybody does it and I just picked it up" (see Romans 12:2). "I'd quit if I could, but I just can't" (see Matthew 19:26; Philippians 4:13).

Some have such a low estimation of themselves that they cannot make a simple statement. Rather they feel they must bolster that statement with some kind of oath. James says, in effect, that our character should be such that our words carry so much weight that it is not necessary to try to strengthen them by vulgarity: "Let your yea be yea; and your nay, nay; lest ye fall into condemnation!"

If we are impatient and quick-tempered and if that impatience shows up frequently in our speech, making a change will not be easy, but neither will it be impossible. Patience is a virtue that is developed over a period of time and requires all the self-discipline we can muster plus the help of God. With God's help, we can become more patient. God never asks the impossible.

## FOR DISCUSSION

1. As time permits, discuss the need for *patience* (Luke 21:19;

Romans 5:4, 5). Give illustrations of the two Greek words used for "patience" in our text.

2. Another vital theme to discuss is the Second Coming; there are over 300 references to this event in the Bible.
3. If you have any farmers (or former farmers) present, they will probably want to expand on the illustration of the patient endurance of the farmer. Note Galatians 6:9 and II Thessalonians 3:13.
4. Skeptical commentators love to comment on phrases like "draweth nigh" in verse 8 to say that Paul, Peter, James, etc., mistakenly thought that Christ would return immediately. Is this true (II Thessalonians 2:2cf.)?
5. Is it true that we often take out our frustrations on those we love the most? What can we do about this tendency?
6. Does it hurt the cause of Christ when we complain about members of the church to others?
7. Contrast the picture of Jesus standing at the door as savior (Revelation 3:20) and Jesus standing at the door as judge (James 5:9).
8. Perhaps assign different ones to survey the life of different prophets to illustrate verse 10. Someone could also report on Job.
9. Compare Jesus' teaching in Matthew 5:33-37 with James 5:12.
10. Does James 5:12 condemn civil oaths? Note Mark 14:62cf.; I Thessalonians 5:27; etc.

# THE POWER OF PRAYER

*James 5:13-18*

We have so many problems. We try to cope from day to day, but sometimes things build up to where we feel like a human pressure cooker. We feel like we want to cry . . . or scream . . . or hit something. But James says we're to be patient (James 5:7). We're not to vent our feelings on others (James 5:9). So what *can* we do? Are we to just keep all these strong feelings bottled up within us? Or is there a legitimate expression for our emotions? James answers, Yes, there is. Today's text begins, "Is any among you afflicted? let him *pray*" (verse 7; emphasis mine). Prayer is mentioned seven times in James 5:13-18. As we study this text, I want to emphasize two things: (1) *Whatever* our situation in life, prayer is always appropriate. (2) There is *power* in prayer.

## I. PRAY ALL THE TIME . . .
### Verses 13-16.

When should we pray? First of all James says: PRAY WHEN THERE'S TROUBLE. Verse 13 begins, "Is any among you afflicted?" "Afflicted" is translated from a term that refers to troubles of all kinds.

Make a list of problems: There are physical problems—

illness, fatigue, and the like. There are psychological problems—turmoil, stress, pressures. There are financial problems—loss of a job, a cut in pay, inflation, increased expenses. There are family problems—problems in our marriage, problems with our children, problems with our parents. There are problems connected with our jobs—a transfer, a move we don't want to make. There are problems connected with how old we are—youthful temptations, middle-age disappointment, old-age frustrations. There are spiritual problems—the inability to live right, a guilty conscience, evil accusations, and so on. All these problems—and any others—are included in the word translated "affliction."

When these problems get us down, what should we do? Apparently some Christians in James' day complained and cursed. Probably the most common reaction today is to worry and fret. James says what we *should* do is *pray*.

It is wonderful to realize that we can pray to a God who understands (Hebrews 4:15, 16), a God who listens and loves. The Psalmist said, "God is our refuge and strength, a very present help in trouble" (Psalm 46:1). He is not an absentee Father who sends a check and says, "Work it out yourself." He is present, He is near, He helps.

But again, James tells us to PRAY WHEN THINGS GO RIGHT. Things don't always go wrong. Sometimes they go right—beautifully right. Maybe we prayed in trouble and God answered our prayers in a wonderful way. Now, instead of feeling bad, we feel good. We have seen how James tells us to express the emotions of sadness and depression. But what if we feel *happy*; how should we express *that* emotion?

In days past rather fanciful and extravagant ways were devised for expressing what some considered to be God-given emotions. In religious services people leaped into the air and shouted. They danced in the aisles. They rolled on the floor. Today such exercises have become more restrained, but there is still a large segment of the religious community that believes that the way to release such emotions is to hold up the hands and wave them repeating aloud phrases like "Hallelujah" and "Praise Jesus." But James prescribes another way to express spiritual joy: "Is any merry? *let him sing psalms*" (verse 13; emphasis mine). The word "merry" means happy, full of joy.

We can go to two extremes regarding prayer. Some of us forget to pray when we have problems. Instead of going to God, we worry. But others of us are quick to pray when trouble comes, but fail to pray when everything is all right, when our prayers have been answered. James covers both possibilities in verse 13: He tells us to pray when things go wrong and he tells us to pray when things go right.

But I can hear someone ask, "Where did you get the idea that we should *pray* when we're happy? My Bible says we should *sing* when we're happy." Let's discuss the phrasing and what is implied by it. The KJV has "let him sing psalms." The writer is speaking of songs of adoration and thanksgiving. The ASV has "let him sing *praise.*"

Singing has always been a natural way to express emotions. There are songs of sadness and songs of happiness. There are songs that reveal the innermost feelings of the heart. And there are songs that express the deepest of spiritual feelings. In Bible times and today, singing has been and is a vital part of our worship of the Most High.

In Ephesians 5:19, 20, we have these instructions concerning singing: "Speaking to yourselves in psalms and hymns and spiritual songs, singing and making melody in your heart to the Lord; giving thanks always for all things unto God and the Father in the name of our Lord Jesus Christ."

There are two directions our songs can go: We can direct them to each other ("speaking to *yourselves* in psalms and hymns and spiritual songs"). Or we can direct our songs to God ("singing and making melody in your heart *to the Lord*"). These last are *prayer* songs, songs of praise and thanksgiving—songs like "We Praise Thee, O God."

It is the latter that is in view of the last part of James 5:13. When we are happy, when things go right, let our minds turn to God. Let us sing songs of praise and adoration and thanksgiving for all our wondrous blessings!

Some can remember when the home was not filled with the discordant noise of the television, radio, and stereo all going simultaneously and full blast. And perhaps some can remember a gray-haired mother going about her daily chores, singing in a clear sweet voice her favorite hymns of praise. To have such a memory is a precious heritage. What kind of heritage of memory are we leaving to *our* children? Will they remember that *we* loved to sing those precious songs of praise and joy?

But then James turns our minds back to the area of troubles as he encourages us to PRAY WHEN THERE'S ILLNESS.

The next three verses—verses 14 through 16—involve some knotty problems. One of the problems is that the subjects of sickness and sin are intertwined and it is not easy to determine which is under consideration at all times. But I do not want the problems of the text to detract from the main thrust of the passage: James is telling us that *whatever* our situation in life, we need to *pray*.

The previous verse spoke of afflictions in general. Now James turns to one of the more common of afflictions, illness. He begins, "Is any sick among you?" Sickness is a problem that affects us all. Most of us do not hesitate to admit that we have had, do have, and will have health problems: From headaches to heart problems, from acne to allergies, from the common cold to cancer, from bursitis to backaches.

What should we do when we're sick? There are many things we should do when illness strikes, but James says that *prayer* is at the top of the list: "Is any sick among you? let him call for the elders of the church; and let them pray over him, anointing him with oil in the name of the Lord: and the prayer of faith shall save the sick, and the Lord shall raise him up" (James 5:14, 15a).

In this passage, the subject of physical illness is the thing under consideration. One of the primary meanings of the word translated "save" is "to heal"—and that is its meaning here. The NASB has "restore," *i.e.*, will restore to health. And the "raising up" mentioned is not a reference to the bodily resurrection from the dead, but rather to the sick person becoming well and getting out of bed. The NEB has "the Lord will raise him from his bed."

There are many things about which we cannot be certain in this passage: Why were the elders to be called? Why was oil used? And what connection does the illness spoken of here have with the sin that is mentioned in the last of verse 15 and in verse 16?

It is my opinion that the healing spoken of here was miraculous. This passage was written at a time when miraculous gifts were a part of God's (temporary) plan (I Corinthians 13:8-10) for the church. One of those miraculous gifts was the gift of healing (I Corinthians 12:9). In those days before the New Testament was complete and readily available, it was the practice of the apostles, as they traveled, to lay their hands on certain ones to impart to them these miraculous gifts (Acts 8:17ff.; 19:6). Thus local congregations could carry on their activities in the absence of an apostle and in the absence of a written book of instructions we call the New Testament. It is my opinion that that is the situation depicted here. The promise of healing seems to be quite definite, which was much more likely to be true in a case of miraculous healing than in simple providential response to prayer.

If my view is correct, one reason the elders could have been called is that they would have been a logical choice to have received the laying-on of the apostles' hands. And if my view is correct, the use of the oil was probably ceremonial or symbolic—similar to its use in anointing a priest, prophet, or king (I Samuel 16:13, etc.). And if all this is true, the situation pictured here is not 100 per cent parallel to our own, since miracles ceased when the New Testament was complete (I Corinthians 13:8-13; James 1:25; etc.).

But we cannot be dogmatic about the healing mentioned here being miraculous. If the healing is *not* miraculous, then the promise of the first part of verse 15 is to be understood as *conditional*—as so many other passages on the power of prayer are: "The prayer of faith shall save [heal] the sick" *if* this is in accordance with the purposes of God. "The Lord shall raise him up [from his sickbed]" *if* we pray according to His will.

Again, if the healing is not miraculous, then one of the reasons the elders were called would have been their character. Verse 16 notes that "the effectual fervent prayer of a *righteous* man availeth much" and if elders are scripturally qualified, they are righteous men (Titus 1:6, 7). Another reason the elders may have been called would be if the physical illness was tied to a *spiritual* problem—as seems to be indicated by the text. In that case, the first need of the individual would have been for spiritual restoration—and then physical healing. For this the spiritual shepherds of the flock would have been eminently qualified.

Further, if the healing was not miraculous, then the oil was probably used medicinally—as it was by the Good Samaritan, who poured oil and wine into the wounds of the man who had been beaten (Luke 10:34). Oil itself is not medicine, but it can promote healing. It feels soothing and, since it is not readily dissolved by water, it serves to cut off exposure to airborne infection.

Having seen some of the challenges of the text, we are on safer ground to affirm that the passage is *not* talking about certain things: For instance, the passage is *not* talking about the ritual called "Extreme Unction," more popularly known as "the last rites." There is no relationship between this manmade "sacrament" and the commandments in our text: In James, it is *elders* who are called, not priests. And in James the purpose of the anointing of the oil and the prayers is to make the person *well*, not prepare him for death.

Again this passage is *not* given to justify the fanciful and flamboyant practices of so-called "faith healers" of today. James does not say to take the sick to a big "healing meeting." He rather says to call men in to pray over him. If men really have the gift of healing today as they claim, the circus-like atmosphere of the big "Holy Ghost rallies" would be totally unnecessary; if men *really* had the gift of healing, they could and would go to the local hospitals and empty them of all their patients—including all terminally ill cancer patients and other incurables. Again, James says to call for the elders of the church, not the "faith healers." Further the faith involved was the faith of the one doing the praying, not the faith of the one prayed over ("let them pray over him . . . and the prayer of faith shall save the sick"); this is mentioned because a common excuse used today, if there is no healing, is that there was a lack of faith on the part of the one who needed the healing.

*But*, we should not let such matters keep us from appreciating the great lessons that James proclaims in this passage:

There is the lesson of the importance of prayer when illness comes. Whether the context is that of the age of miracles or whether it is not, the lesson is still the same: When there is illness, we should pray to God. The body of the child of God is called "the temple of the Holy Spirit" (I Corinthians 6:19ff.) and we are taught to be concerned about it. When Hezekiah was ill, he prayed and God heard his prayer (II Kings 2). Epaphroditus "was sick nigh unto death: but God had mercy on him" (Philippians 2:27).

All healing is divine—not miraculous today, but still divine. Over the main portal of the Presbyterian Medical Center in Manhattan, New York, are inscribed these words: "All healing is of God; physicians only bind up the wounds." This is no longer the age of miracles, but that is not to say that God does not hear and answer prayer. God does not work contrary to natural law (*i.e.*, miraculously), but He does work *through* His laws of nature (*i.e.*, providentially).

But we need also to learn to pray, as did Jesus, "Not my will, but thine be done" (Luke 22:42). Rather than remove the illness, God may give us the grace to bear it, as He did in the case of Paul (II Corinthians 12:8, 9cf.). But regardless of God's answer, the lesson in James 5:14 is that we should pray for the sick.

A second lesson is that in the case of illness, God expects us to do what *we* can. James says to call for the elders, oil is to be used, and so forth. We cannot be dogmatic about the purpose of the oil, but it had *some* purpose, and no doubt James' readers knew what that purpose was. They would have understood that God does not do for us what we can do for ourselves.

There is nothing in the Bible that goes contrary to modern medical practices, as long as those practices are ethical and right within themselves. Luke "the beloved physician" (Colossians 4:14) worked side by side with Paul, who performed miracles. There are many accounts in the Bible of "medicine" being used (Luke 10:34cf.) and even recommended (I Timothy 5:23). Each medical breakthrough is a blessing from God Himself, the source of "every good . . . and . . . perfect gift" (James 1:17)!

Another lesson is the importance of the work of elders. Whether I understand all the implications of the command or not, James says when there is illness, one should call for the *elders* of the church.

Elders are the leaders of the local congregations (Acts 20:17). They are also known as the bishops (or overseers) and pastors (shepherds) of the flock (Acts 20:17, 28; I Peter 5:1-4; Titus 1:5, 7). They have been given the oversight of the local congregation. We are to respect them and follow their leadership (Hebrews 13:17). As the shepherds of our souls, it should be the most natural thing in the world to turn to them when trouble comes into our lives!

Now James adds this thought: PRAY WHEN THERE'S

SIN. At first glance, James seems to change the subject abruptly. After saying that the prayer of faith shall save the sick, the writer adds, "And if he have committed *sins*, they shall be forgiven him" (verse 15; emphasis mine).

It is the blending of the teaching on sickness and sin that challenges our thinking. Possibly all that James is trying to get across is that the spiritual man should not be neglected in our concern for the physical man. If the person who was sick also had spiritual problems, those too should be disposed of. After all, spiritual health is much more important than physical health.

It is also possible that James is acknowledging the fact that many do not become concerned about their spiritual condition until their physical lives are threatened. When that is the case, *then* they are more likely to call for the elders and not only ask for prayers for their illnesses, but also for forgiveness of their sins.

And it is even possible that James is suggesting some connection between the sin referred to and the sickness! A life of habitual, continual sin can dissipate and harm the body. I'm not suggesting that all sickness is a result of personal sin, that there is always a connection between sin and sickness. The disciples made the mistake of thinking that (John 9:2, 3). Paul's "thorn in the flesh" was not the result of personal sin, but rather was to keep him humble (II Corinthians 12:7cf.).

But *sometimes* there is a connection between specific sins and specific illnesses. A common illustration is that of certain health problems related to sexual promiscuity, such as venereal diseases (Romans 1:27). A recent illustration of this type of thing has been the herpes epidemic largely spread by unscriptural sexual activity. The most recent illustration is the concern about AIDS—the Acquired Immune Deficiency Syndrome. Seventy percent of those with AIDS are male homosexuals. One homosexual sadly said, "It looks like we may have to choose between our lifestyle and life itself."

Psalm 32 is a good illustration of the possible relationship of sin and sickness, especially when we fail to repent. In verses 3 and 4, David speaks of the physical, emotional, and spiritual agony he went through as long as he tried to conceal his sin. He aged overnight. He had constant aches and pains. He couldn't sleep. He became weak.

But to return to our text: When sin (and its consequences) is in our life, what should we do? Many things, but again James stresses that near the top of the list is *prayer*. In Acts 8, the apostle Peter commanded *the sinner himself* to pray (verse 22). Now James adds the thought of praying *for each other* when we sin: "Confess your faults one to another, and pray one for another, that ye may be healed. The effectual fervent prayer of a righteous man availeth much" (James 5:16).

It is significant that the prayer spoken of here is preceded by confession. Confession is good for the soul. Like an abscess deep within the body, unacknowledged sin can poison both mind and body—and, like the abscess, often there is the need to expose and drain the source of infection. A moment ago we referred to David's agony as long as he attempted to cover his sin. How did he find relief? Notice verse 5 in Psalm 32: "*I acknowledged my sin* unto thee, and mine iniquity have I not hid. I said, I will confess my transgressions unto the Lord; and thou forgavest the iniquity of my sin." (Emphasis mine.)

But whether there are physical and emotional consequences to our sins or not, confession is still of great value (Proverbs 28:13; Matthew 3:6)—to combat pride if for no other reason (I John 2:16). The first One to whom we should confess our sins is God (I John 1:9). But James stresses that there is also value in confessing *to each another.* This is *not* referring to the Auricular Confession. "Auricular" means "in the ear." Auricular Confession refers to the confession of sins "in the ear" of a priest in the confessional box. But James 5:16 doesn't say that we should confess to a priest, but rather to one another, nor in a box but in a situation of mutual trust and concern.

What are we to confess? We are to confess our sins. The Amplified version expands the word "faults" in its translation: "your slips, your false steps, your offenses, your sins." Don't confess, "*If* I have sinned, I'm sorry." Confess that you *have* sinned.

This command ties in with what we generally call "a public confession"; it shows that such an action is permissible and can be beneficial. Guy N. Woods, in his commentary on James, underlines this point with these words:

> We are to pray one for another. We may, however, effectively do so, only when a brother confesses his sins and turns away from them. (I John 5:16) ... It is necessary in the nature of the case that those who have known of the sins should have equal knowledge of the penitence. But, this we can know only through a confession of the brother involved. It is, therefore, a practical rule that the confession should be as public as is the sin (p. 305).

A public confession of sins lets many know of our penitence—and gains for us the benefit of the prayer of many righteous souls.

But we would be doing the passage an injustice to limit it to a public confession. The passage is first and foremost pointing up the need for mutual confession and mutual prayer. Each of us has the need for others with whom we can be completely open—ones with whom we can unburden our souls and share our loads (Galatians 6:2). Many of us have found such a person in a loving Christian mate. Others have found a good Christian friend that helps and strengthens them.

But to return to the main theme, James says, "And *pray* one for another, that ye may be healed." Again there is disagreement over whether the healing spoken of here is physical or spiritual. But whether physical or spiritual, the bottom line is the same. If the healing is physical, forgiveness of sins is *implicitly* promised. If the healing is spiritual, forgiveness of sins is *explicitly* promised.

The point being made is that *there is power in prayer*. If preceded by the proper conditions, prayer has power to help the body and free the soul. Which introduces us to the second main point of our text:

## II. . . . BECAUSE PRAYER IS POWERFUL.
### Verses 16-18.

The last of verse 16 says, "The effectual fervent prayer of a righteous man availeth much." This is a great passage on the power of prayer. The prayer of a righteous man is said to be "effectual" ("effective"). But further, this "effectual" prayer "*avails*." But it not only avails, it "avails *much*."

Every word of this passage is packed with meaning. The *person* whose prayer is powerful is "a righteous man." James doesn't say the prayer of an eloquent preacher is powerful nor the prayer of a noted church leader. Rather he says that the prayer of a *righteous* man is powerful. That man may be unassuming, his prayers may not be eloquent, but if he is a Christian and his life is right, his prayers are powerful!

The *kind* of prayer that is powerful is described as "*fervent* prayer." If our prayers are to have power, we must get serious about praying!

Then we have the words that emphasize how much potential power prayer has. The word "effectual" is translated from the Greek word from which we get the English word "energy." Prayer can energize our lives. A life without prayer is like a car without fuel. A $10,000 car without energy in the tank is of little value; put some energy in the tank and, all other things being equal, it can take you 100,000 miles.

Then there are the words "availeth much." "Availeth"

comes from a Greek word that means "is strong" or power-ful. "Much" means "very." So "availeth much" means "is *very* strong."

Not long ago I did extensive reading on this passage in various commentaries and study books. Much of what I read left me greatly dissatisfied—for so many of the writers seemed to be more concerned with human psychology than with divine intervention. The Bible teaches that God does not work miraculously today in this world, but at the same time, the Bible teaches that God *does* work, that He *is* active (Romans 8:28). And it teaches that He responds to our prayers as a loving father responds to the requests of his children (Matthew 7:11). I may not know and understand all that is involved in God answering my prayers, but I know He does. And this is enough for me to know. I know prayer is powerful!

To impress this indelibly on our hearts, James gives an illustration from the Old Testament, an illustration of a righteous man whose prayer availed much: "Elias [Elijah] was a man subject to like passions as we are, and he prayed earnestly that it might not rain and it rained not on the earth by the space of three years and six months. And he prayed again, and the heaven gave rain, and the earth brought forth her fruit" (James 5:17, 18).

You will want to read the full story in I Kings 17 and 18. It is climaxed by the classic confrontation of Elijah and the prophets of Baal, with the fire of God consuming the prophet's sacrifice, the altar it was on, and even the water in the trench surrounding it. The people fell on their faces and cried, "The Lord, he is the God; the Lord, he is the God" (I Kings 18:39). Following that Elijah prayed for rain to break the three-year drought. First Kings 18:45 says: "And it came to pass . . . that the heaven was black with clouds and wind, and there was a great rain"! It is an amazing story demonstrating the power of God—and James stresses that at the heart of it is *prayer*.

But someone may object, "I don't see how there can be a

parallel here with *my* prayer life. After all Elijah was a very unusual person. He was a prophet of God and endued with special powers." James anticipates such an objection for he begins verse 17 by saying, "[Elijah] was a man subject to like passions [or feelings] *as we are.*" In the 400 years between Malachi and the coming of Christ, the Jews had developed an exaggerated concept of Elijah, making him a mysteriously heavenly figure. James says that such a view was incorrect. He was a righteous man, but he wasn't perfect. He had the same emotions we have—and the same weaknesses.

Why then was Elijah's prayer powerful? Because he was *the kind of person* whose prayers are powerful—the "righteous" man of verse 16. The text says "he prayed *earnestly* that it might not rain." In the original language a Hebrew figure of speech is used. The passage literally says, "he prayed *with prayer.*" Elijah really prayed, prayed with all his being.

For what did he pray? "He prayed earnestly that it might not rain." This gives us a detail that we don't get from I Kings 17. James lets us know that the drought not only ended with prayer, it also began with prayer. And how powerful was that prayer? "It rained not on the earth by the space of three years and six months." Here was a prayer so powerful that it affected the weather of the area—and thus the entire economic structure—for three and one-half years! That's some prayer! Then James says, "And he prayed *again*, and the heaven gave rain." As a matter of fact he prayed at least seven times; he was persistent in prayer. "And the earth brought forth her fruit" (verse 18).

Why did James choose this particular illustration of the power of prayer? It was spectacular, but so were many other Old Testament examples of answered prayer. I like to think that James chose this specific example because it is more an illustration of providence than the miraculous—in other words God working *through* natural law (as He does today) rather than contrary to natural law. The rain did not come from a clear sky; it came from a cloud. The cloud did not appear instantaneously; it came from the sea, the Mediterranean Sea, and grew. That's the way rain came in that area. The hot winds from the east and south brought drought, but the west wind brought the moisture from the Mediterranean Sea and refreshed the land.

This is *not* primarily written to encourage us to have prayer meetings in dry weather. Not that that is a bad idea, but this is rather written to encourage us to pray *all* the time, to pray everywhere, to pray under every circumstance—because there is power in prayer! Even though it is not the age of miracles, God can still work through natural law to answer our prayers!

## FOR DISCUSSION

1. Do Christians have problems? What problems are mentioned in James 5? Why doesn't God make His children immune to problems?
2. As time permits, discuss the subject of prayer. Look at the words of the song "Pray In the Morning"—and perhaps sing it together.
3. A. T. Robertson says that the word "affliction" in verse 13 includes the "natural depression" that comes as a result of such misfortunes. Is depression a widespread problem today? What resources does a Christian have to deal with this problem?
4. The Greek word translated "sing psalms" is *psallo*. If it is appropriate, you may want to discuss this word. A *Cappella Music* by Ferguson would be a good source book.
5. Go through a song book and pick out songs that are *teaching* songs and songs that are *prayer* songs.
6. A thought question: When we are happy, are we more likely to sing a song of praise to God—or the latest "pop" (or country-and-western) song??
7. As time permits, discuss the "health and wealth" TV evangelists of today—and how they differ from the simple instruc-

tions in James 5:14-16.

8. Should we pray when there is illness (II Samuel 12; II Corinthians 12:8cf.; etc.)? Should we always expect God to answer "yes" to such prayers? Why would God sometimes answer "no"?

9. Does James say that in case of illness, we should first of all call for the *preacher*? Have we developed a denominational "pastor" concept regarding the preacher?

10. Can some sins affect us physically? Think about sins such as worry, anger, and bitterness.

11. Discuss the matter of public confession for sin: When it is needed and when it is not—and how it should be done.

12. Has prayer ever helped you? Give the class one specific example of how you have been helped through prayer.

# THE NEED FOR
# SOUL-CONSERVATION

*James 5:19, 20*

We come to the close of
our study of the book of James. It has been a fairly leisurely
journey, but one does not rush through an art gallery that
contains nothing but masterpieces. I have not exhausted the
great themes in this book, but I have at least tried to touch
on the multiplicity of truths contained therein.

In our last lesson, James indicated that there must be
concern for any who are sick, whether physically or spiritually (James 5:15, 16). In the last two verses of the book,
his primary concern is for the spiritually ill: "Brethren, if
any of you do err from the truth, and one convert him; let
him know, that he which converteth the sinner from the
error of his way, shall save a soul from death, and shall hide
a multitude of sins" (James 5:19, 20).

When I was a boy, many agriculturists were concerned
about soil conservation. Natural cover had been stripped
from the earth, poor farming methods had depleted the
soil, and rain and wind were eroding the soil at a rapid rate.
Much of the vital topsoil had already been lost and ever-
widening gullies scarred land that had become good only
for inferior pasture. Since all physical life on earth was
dependent on two or three inches of topsoil, a disaster of
monumental proportions was in the making!

Some started a campaign for soil conservation based on

the familiar call for help: S.O.S. Their slogan was "Save Our Soil!" Gradually farmers learned terracing, contour farming, crop rotation, the planting of windbreaks, fertilization, and other practices that protected the soil and also returned to it the vital nutrients that were taken out. Disaster was averted, at least for the moment.

As I have grown older, and gotten more involved in the work of the church, I have discovered a continuing disaster of greater proportions and more drastic consequences than that faced by farmers thirty-five years ago. It is the loss of those who once were faithful members of the church. Some have estimated that over a period of time we lose up to 50 per cent of those who are baptized into Christ. Whatever the figure, it is too high! Our need today is for SOUL-conservation. The silent S.O.S. of the multitudes is "Save Our Souls!"

## I. IT IS POSSIBLE FOR A CHILD OF GOD TO GO ASTRAY.

The first lesson we learn from our text is that it is possible for a child of God to so sin as to be lost. Some deny this. One individual wrote a booklet entitled, "Do a Christian's Sins Damn His Soul?" in which he said:

> We take a position that a Christian's sins do not damn his soul. The way a Christian lives, what he says, his character, his conduct, or his attitude toward other people have nothing whatever to do with the salvation of his soul. . . . All the sins he may commit from idolatry to murder will not make his soul in any more danger.

Such an attitude goes contrary to the teaching of both the Old Testament (I Chronicles 28:9) and the New Testament. Passages could be multiplied to show the possibility of a child of God being lost. Christians are told that they can fall (I Corinthians 10:12), that they can fall from grace (Galatians 5:4), that they can become castaways (I Corinthians 9:27), that if they sin willfully they have rejected the sacrifice of Christ (Hebrews 10:26). But no passage teaches this more powerfully than our text.

James begins, "*Brethren*, if any of *you* do err from the truth, . . ." The individual under consideration is not an alien sinner, but an erring brother in Christ—a child of God who has sinned, a Christian who is not right with the Lord.

The Greek word translated "err" means "to wander, to go astray"—as on a mountain peak, or as one who has missed the path. The NASB has "if any among you *strays* from the truth." The picture is not that of open rebellion against God, but a gradual drifting away from God and the things of God—as a sheep might wander from the fold and become lost.

We are not told whether the error was in life, in teaching, or both. It is possible that James was especially concerned about doctrinal error. There was always the temptation for Jewish Christians to return to the tenants of the old law (see Hebrews 2:1ff.; 6:4-8; 10:25ff.; etc.). But such a doctrinal departure invariably affects one's life. So the distinction is not important.

The key thing is that they wandered from *the truth*. Only the truth can make us free (John 8:32). Only the truth purifies the soul (I Peter 1:22). And that truth is found in God's word (John 17:17). The most important thing we can do to discourage people from straying spiritually is to preach and teach the truth—the whole truth, the positive side and the negative side of the truth, nothing but the truth.

What is the destination of those who depart from the truth and are not brought back? "He which converteth the sinner from the error of his way shall save a soul from *death*." This is not speaking of physical death, for repentance cannot spare us that appointment (Hebrews 9:27). The "death" spoken of here can only refer to *spiritual* death—being separated from God in this life (Isaiah 49:1, 2; I Timothy 5:6), but especially separated from God throughout eternity if there is no repentance (Revelation 20:15cf.)!

If we fully appreciated this, we would make a greater effort to keep it from happening. In our soulwinning activities, too often we "dip them and then drop them." We "compass sea and land" to make one convert and then, when he is made, we "make him twofold more the child of hell" than he was before (Matthew 23:15) by failing to continue teaching him "to observe all things" the Lord has commanded (Matthew 28:20). Too many of us want to assist at the birth of a new life in Christ (John 3:5; I Peter 1:23), and then deny any responsibility for the spiritual baby. Let us give these precious souls the continued support of love, concern, help, continued teaching—for if they move away from that commitment they will be lost, lost eternally!

At this moment there are dozens, hundreds, of erring Christians within a few miles of where you live and where you worship—on their way to eternal *death*—and until we face such facts squarely we will never be sufficiently motivated to try to bring them back!

If a child were lost in the woods, hundreds would turn out—and no one would rest until that child was either found or hope was gone. But a child of God can be lost spiritually and few of us are concerned! Someone with a rare disease can capture the attention of the nation and thousands will give money, time, and energy to save that life—but one can be at the point of *spiritual* death and we do not get excited!


## II. IT IS POSSIBLE TO BRING THE ERRING CHILD BACK.

But the main thrust of these verses is not negative, but

positive. The emphasis is not that a child of God can be lost, but that there is *hope*. That erring child can be brought back! Spiritual death can be averted! A multitude of sins can be hidden! "If any do err from the truth, and one *convert* him; let him know that he which *converteth* the sinner from the error of his way shall save a soul from death."

The word translated "convert" primarily means "to turn." The NASB has "he who *turns the sinner* from the error of his way will save his soul from death." The RSV has "whoever *brings back* a sinner from the error of his way shall save his soul from death." These indicate the possibility of bringing the erring child back to the Lord and His way. For this we thank God. These verses are filled with hope!

This does not mean that we can restore every unfaithful Christian. There are many who are hardened and intent on going their own way (Hebrews 6:1-6). There are those who will reject our overtures of love again and again and again— so that at some point good sense will dictate that our time can be spent more profitably with those who are responsive (Matthew 7:6). But there are many who would be, will be, receptive IF we will but show love and concern. Our greatest sin is not in wasting our time talking to and teaching the unresponsive, but in *failing* to talk to those who *would* respond if we put forth the effort.

When a brother becomes unfaithful, there are a number of ways we can react: We can ignore the problem and do nothing. We can give up on him in disgust—and wash our hands of all responsibility. We can treat him harshly—and drive him further into sin. Or we can go to him in love and try to bring him back in meekness and fear. The last is the challenge given to us by Paul:

"Brethren, if a man be overtaken in a fault, ye which are spiritual, restore such an one in a spirit of meekness; considering thyself, lest thou also be tempted. Bear ye one another's burdens, and so fulfill the law of Christ" (Galatians 6:1, 2).

We improve our chances of bringing the lost back if we go to them in *the right way*. Paul says, "In a spirit of meekness." Our text does not go into detail concerning the way we are to treat the erring, but there are suggestions in the text. Note the last phrase in the passage: "*Shall hide a multitude of sins*." James is probably referring to Proverbs 10:12: "Hatred stirreth up strife but *love* covereth all sins." (Emphasis mine.) To accomplish what we want to accomplish, we need to go to the unfaithful in *love*.

How can we express that love so that only good results? First, *show* them that you still care for them. Be interested in them. Go by to see them. Invite them into your home for a meal. Especially take advantage of times of emotional stress. Help them when there are times of happiness and sorrow—births, deaths, marriages, successes, and failures.

Second, *talk* to them about their spiritual needs (note Hebrews 10:24; II Timothy 4:2). Love is an attitude of heart that *seeks the best* for the one loved. A parent who does not correct his child does not love his child (Hebrews 12:6cf.). If we are not willing to do a little serious talking to the erring, we do not love them! In fact, many unfaithful members know that we are *supposed* to talk to them, and will hold it against us if we are not straightforward with them.

When we do talk to an erring brother, we must say what *that* person needs. Some have been thoroughly taught in days past and just need to be reminded of the blessings they are missing and of the consequences of their unfaithfulness. But others have "need that one teach [them] again which be the first principles of the oracles of God" (Hebrews 5:12). They wandered from the faith because they were not well grounded in the first place; we did not continue the discipling process after baptism (Matthew 28:19, 20). To go to such and simply say, "We missed you and hope you'll come back!" is as misplaced as the proverbial pork chop at a synagogue! These folks need to be *taught*, not merely exhorted!

A third way we can show love for the erring is to *pray* for them (James 5:15, 16). Let us not hesitate to let our weaker brothers and sisters *know* that we love them and are praying for them. If we really *love* our fellow Christians, it will show and *it will have an effect.*

## III. IT IS OUR RESPONSIBILITY TO TRY TO BRING THE ERRING CHILD BACK.

The passage begins, "*Brethren, if any of you. . . .*" The one involved in bringing back the erring is another child of God. Paul said in Galatians 6:1: "*Brethren, if a man be overtaken in a fault, ye which are spiritual,* restore such an one in the spirit of meekness." (Emphasis mine.) It is *our* responsibility to try to bring the erring child back. The world is not interested in bringing the erring back. The denominational world cannot do it. Unfaithful Christians are not going to do it. If faithful Christians do not do it, it will not be done.

This is not to say that the unfaithful have no responsibility, that if they are lost, they can point a finger at everyone else and say, "*You* failed me; it is all *your* fault." God made us all free moral agents, responsible for our own destiny. Whether other people treat me right or not, *I* should still act right. If I become unfaithful, whether anyone encourages me to be restored or not, I will still have to face God and give an account of my unfaithfulness. *But,* let me still insist that the rest of us *also* have a responsibility—to do all we can to bring the wandering home.

In the texts we have read, this responsibility comes to us as a *command* from Almighty God. But there are also many reasons we should *want* to try to restore the erring. First and foremost, he is our *brother.* I am reminded of the boy who carried a younger boy on his back to a boy's home. Someone offered to relieve the older boy of his load. His reply has become a classic: "Naw. He ain't heavy. *He's my brother.*" This truth needs to reach more than our ears and minds; it needs to reach our *hearts:* The ones of whom we are speaking are our brothers and sisters in Christ. These are those for whom Christ died.

Again, we should want to try to restore the erring because *it could happen to us.* This is implied: "Brethren, if any of *you* do err from the truth." And this possibility is specifically stated in I Corinthians 10:12: "Wherefore let him that thinketh he standeth take heed lest he fall." Being aware of this possibility, ask yourself this question, "If it was *I* that had gone astray, would I want my fellow Christians to be concerned, to try to help me?" If your answer is a resounding "yes," then remember the Golden Rule (Matthew 7:12)!

Further we should want to try to restore the erring because of *what God has done for us.* Our souls have been saved from death; a multitude of *our* sins have been hidden by the blood of Christ; we should want that for all men—whether without or within the church (II Corinthians 1:4). God has blessed us and forgiven us; let's *share* that.

There are many reasons why we should want to try to restore the erring. There is the negative *influence* the erring can have—and there is the *joy* of having a part in bringing a lost brother or sister home. But surely the most impelling reason is because our efforts can make the difference in whether they are *saved* or *lost:* "Shall save a soul from *death,* and shall hide a multitude of sins."

It is tragic not to have one's sins hidden or covered. In Nehemiah 4:5, Nehemiah speaks to God about Sanballat and Tobiah: "Cover not their iniquity"—in other words, *remember* their sins. What a chilling thought. But, on the other hand, what a blessing to have one's sins covered and forgiven! The Psalmist spoke of this in Psalm 85:2, "Thou hast forgiven the iniquity of thy people, thou hast covered all their sin."

To have one's sins hidden is to have them forgiven as they are covered by the blood of Christ (I John 1:7, 9).

Surely the potential salvation of another soul should be sufficient motivation to get busy trying to restore the erring!

But, as we think about reasons why we should *want* to win back the unfaithful, let me list one more: Because our attitude toward the lost can be a vital factor in *our own* salvation.

Consider this question very seriously: What kind of shape are our souls in if we are not even *concerned* about others in our spiritual family who are lost in sin?! Can it be that we, like the elder brother in Luke 15, are more concerned about *our* rights and privileges, than we are about those who have gone into "the far country" of sin?

There is a vital relationship between *our* salvation and the salvation of those we have an opportunity to teach. In I Timothy 4:16, Paul challenged Timothy to take heed to himself and his teaching and to continue in them, "for in so doing this thou shall *both* save thyself *and* them that hear thee." (Emphasis mine.)

To help each of us consider the state of his or her heart, let's close this lesson with a self-examination:

---

AM I CONCERNED ABOUT OTHERS?

1. Am I trying to save a soul this year?　　Yes ( )　No ( )

2. Do I pray daily for specific ones that are lost?　　Yes ( )　No ( )

3. Have I talked to anyone about his or her soul in the last month?　　Yes ( )　No ( )

4. When someone obeys the gospel or is restored, do I make a special point of meeting that person?　　Yes ( )　No ( )

---

5. Do I try to visit and get acquainted with all new members?  Yes ( )  No ( )

6. Have I ever taken a new member "under my wing" and helped him or her to grow?  Yes ( )  No ( )

7. Am I concerned when members of the church stop attending as they should?  Yes ( )  No ( )

8. When a member begins to show a lack of interest, do I go *at once* to see what I can do?  Yes ( )  No ( )

9. Do I go out of my way to show out-of-duty members that I still love them and am concerned about them?  Yes ( )  No ( )

10. Have I *ever* encouraged an unfaithful Christian to be restored?  Yes ( )  No ( )

Thus James ends his letter. There are no greetings, no benedictions, no formal closing, no words of farewell. To the end James remains practical, pertinent, and challenging.

## FOR DISCUSSION

1. It might be worthwhile to begin with a review of the great teachings in James. Will *learning* these truths do us any good if we do not *obey* them (James 1:22; 2:26; 4:17)?

2. Do you see any significance in the fact that James closes the book with the theme of reclaiming lost Christians? Why do

you suppose there are no final greetings as there are in most of the New Testament letters?

3. Should we be more concerned about the *physical* need of others, or the *spiritual*? Yet on which do we often seem to put the most emphasis?

4. Discuss our responsibility to new converts. *Is* it true that sometimes we "dip them and then drop them"?

5. As time permits, discuss what the Bible teaches about "the possibility of apostasy." You may want to compile a list of scriptures to show that a child of God *can* so sin as to be lost.

6. Are we obligated to work indefinitely at restoring a certain one if that one never gives us the slightest bit of encouragement? Would you say, however, that usually our greater mistake is that of putting forth *too much* or *too little* effort to restore a specific lost soul?

7. The author suggests that many times the need of the erring is not merely to be exhorted to return, but to rather be re-taught. Do you agree or disagree with this?

8. Give as many reasons as possible why *every* Christian should be trying to restore the erring. How does the Golden Rule tie in with this?

9. Is it true that often we wait *so long* to go to the unfaithful, when we do finally go, little can be accomplished? How can we correct this?

10. Close with a challenge: During the next week, *each* class member talk to at least *one* erring Christian—to encourage him or her to return. Discuss the results the following week.